GET YOUR
HIGHEST PRICE:

*Power Marketing
for
Luxury Homeowners*

DAVID & LINDA MICHONSKI

Other products that might interest you

- For a Free **Directory of Market Experts**
  Go to *http://GetYourHighestPrice.com/Directory*

- For a Free **Quarterly Market Report on the US market**
  Email us at: *Report@PowerMarketing.pro*

- To purchase a subscription to the **Core Value Pricing Calculator**
  Go to: *http://GetYourHighestPrice.com/CoreValue*

- To purchase a subscription to the **Home Value Appreciator**
  Go to *http://GetYourHighestPrice.com/HomeApp*

Copyright © 2013 David & Linda Michonski
All rights reserved.

ISBN: 1480027332
ISBN-13: 9781480027336

For our friends and clients
(known and unknown)

Table of Contents

Chapter 1: Learning what to do (and why) from the psychology of an auction. 1

Chapter 2: Challenges to reaching your goal 17

Chapter 3: The *Power Marketing* solution. 29

Chapter 4: Seven step pricing – no fingers in the air 43

Chapter 5: How marketing gets the highest price. 61

Chapter 6: How to hire an agent 73

Chapter 7: Agent marketing tools 93

Chapter 8: Qualifying buyers 121

Chapter 9: Business essentials of a luxury listing contract 127

Chapter 10: For Sale by Owner (FSBO). 147

Chapter 11: Paying a higher commission and why you might 153

Chapter 12: Sales that explain it all: *Le Domaine Résistance* 161

Chapter 13: Sales that explain it all: Clarendon Court 181

Appendix 1: Why "average" vs. "median" price. 201

Introduction

This book will empower you, the luxury homeowner, to get the highest price for your luxury home. We even make this outrageous suggestion: if you follow our advice, for every million dollars of value in your property, you should get about $50,000 extra (and possibly much more). Because the strategies and techniques suggested here should add so much value, they might even pay for your agent's commission several times over.

What we mean by this amazing claim is that these actions (which we term *power marketing*) will empower you not only to hire a good agent who can create a true market for your property and thereby unlock its maximum value, but in addition, you will acquire the know-how to hold your agent's feet to the fire. By empowering you with what you need to know, you can drive the real estate brokerage industry to better performance and enhance the marketing skills of agents everywhere. This should have the sanguine result of your netting a higher price. Indeed, we have seen these actions repeatedly get more for sellers and have provided real-life examples throughout the book, especially in the stories found in Chapters 12 and 13.

These actions work because they, like all the strategies and techniques underlying *power marketing*, are based on human nature and are largely unchanging and not trend-dependent. *Power marketing* begins with the premise that the luxury buyer is just as smart as you, the luxury seller. You must respect their success and intelligence and give them a reason to act and to pay more. The luxury market's tiny size and illiquidity breeds buyers lacking urgency to act because they can afford to wait. It acknowledges that luxury pricing is highly subjective and inexact. As a result, the price you get will largely be due to the marketing and marketer you employ.

Because *power marketing* holds the highest respect for the intelligence of the buyer you are targeting, it is not about gimmicks, nor about pulling the wool over a buyer's eyes. After all, the buyer you are seeking is likely to be one of the smartest and most successful people in the world. Rather, *power marketing* is all about understanding what drives a luxury buyer to act so that you can influence their actions. That means you and your agent can have greater influence over the sales and marketing process.

Once you grasp *power marketing*, you will know the fastest and most profitable way to sell your luxury home. You will also have the power to sell any real estate in any market, at any time. In fact, *power marketing* can dramatically increase the price you get for anything.

Come, and let us show you how.

David & Linda Michonski
Greenwich, Connecticut

Acknowledgements

As real estate professionals, friends often ask our advice on selling their luxury real estate. To answer their questions, we decided to create this easy-to-read book. They, in turn, helped us enormously in getting it written.

Anne Beaty shrunk the manuscript by 20% without losing a thought and brought simplicity and directness. Cynthia Canaday walked us out of literary dead-ends and kept us focused on clarity of thinking. Bill Baugham helped with diction and grammar. All provided often needed encouragement to finish the book and get it into the hands of luxury consumers. When it is time for each of our friends to sell their luxury home, we hope they are now better positioned to get the best price.

We are also grateful to John Coburn, G. Wade Staniar, and Robert R. Borden III, now or formerly of LandVest in Boston whose collective wisdom provided all the initial insights that have matured into *power marketing*.

Our former clients allowed us the privileged opportunity to sell their homes and gain the valuable experiences found here. To all of them, too numerous to single out, this book is our way of saying 'thank you.'

Chapter 1: Learning what to do (and why) from the psychology of an auction

Question: Do you know how to get the highest price for your home? The answer is to create a competitive moment in time when you have multiple buyers bidding simultaneously (a "market"), willingly, gladly, and perhaps even enthusiastically.

Now a second question: Do you know how to create that competitive moment in time? That market? If you know the answer, put down this book and read something else. If not, keep reading. This book will tell you.

Selling a home involves many elements: hiring an agent, pricing the property, demonstrating value to buyers, finding buyers, removing obstructions to their bidding, negotiating a deal and closing the buyer. Nothing new here.

But as a luxury homeowner, you face challenges most homeowners do not: (1) a very small market, (2) illiquidity in that small market, (3) pricing a property that you probably created to be unique and incomparable, (4) the smartest buyers, sophisticated and tough, who, because they are also rich, (5) lack an urgency to act and can afford to wait. To overcome these additional challenges, you need a different kind of marketing, *power marketing*.

To grasp it, let's begin at the end, your goal. Envision a moment in time when you can indeed get the highest price. Imagine yourself in the room of a luxury auction house looking to sell a painting, furniture or jewelry. Then imagine a hundred hands in the air, all bidding enthusiastically for your item. In fact, imagine each buyer trying to outbid the other.

Isn't this moment the goal of every luxury seller? Doesn't getting to it virtually guarantee the highest price the market will bear? Keep this image of the luxury auction in your mind for the next few pages as we walk you through what happens. By taking you into the auction room, you will see all the elements, principles, strategies and circumstances needed to sell your property for the highest price. The rest of this book is about the details along the way.

The preliminary preparations

Let's imagine the preliminary steps of selling at auction. First, you took the object to the auction house (or they may have come to your home). The auction house immediately assigned the project to a specialist. For example, if you have a piece of 18th Century New England furniture, they will assign you the person who specializes in that. Similarly, if you have Chinese porcelain they will assign that specialist. Specialists are often researchers who know not just all about that object, but also about the market for that object. They help the auction house to determine the potential size of the market and who buys this kind of item. The researcher/specialist then evaluates the object by researching its provenance, how many similar objects sold in the past, for how much and whether your object has rarity, celebrity or historic value. They consider its condition: Is it worn? Can it still be used?

Once the specialist has done their research and determined what prices have been achieved in the past and who the potential market for the property is today, the specialist turns their attention to price. He or she does not, however, give you a specific price, but rather a likely valuation range. This is called "band pricing" and is common to the auction. It is imprecise because the ultimate selling price is determined at the auction. The only price fixed in advance is the floor price, the price below which you will not sell. Note that in contrast to the auctioneer, the real estate agent does not give a range of value, but rather sets a price and the price the agent sets is the highest price.

The auctioneer also does not print a price in the program, again unlike the real estate agent who prints a price on a brochure or listing sheet. Instead, the auctioneer gives an estimated range of value, with the hope of exceeding that range. By not printing the highest possible price, the auctioneer strives to get buyers comfortable with a defensible range of value (we will deal with this in Chapter 4 on Pricing). Then, when buyers are comfortable with the range of value, they bid, sometimes above it.

From a marketing point of view, the price the auctioneer gets is determined by factors beyond just the object's estimated value. It depends also on how many buyers are in the room at the time of auction and how well the auctioneer orchestrates those bidders. Unlike the real estate agent, the auctioneer's role is not to get the asking price. Instead, it is to create a market for the object. Once created, the auctioneer relies on that market and his marketing skill at orchestrating it to get the highest possible price.

The auctioneer also does not stand at the podium explaining her appraisals or her valuation of the object the way a real estate agent is forced to do. The reason is at the core of *power marketing*. A savvy, logical buyer's response should be: Do you have anyone who will pay that? If the auctioneer does, the value is validated. If not, the defensive valuation explanation alone will not prompt a bid.

To illustrate, join us in a fictional auction room where a luxury object valued at between $5M and $6M is about to be auctioned. We have added side notes to call your attention to key moments in getting the highest price.

Going to an auction

The auction is always mesmerizing with the auctioneer, barking and shouting.

"Do I have a starting bid of two million?" he bellows as dozens of buyers wave paddles in the air, enticed by an opening bid way under the likely valuation range of $5M to $6M. Pulses start to race.

Within seconds the bidding rises to two and a half million dollars, then three million, three and a half million, four million, four and a half million. The competition weakens if not disables the bargain hunters. Those with the financial power to win take center stage. With so many bidders now clamoring for the same prize, buyers become fearless.

"The current bid is four and a half million dollars. Do I hear five million dollars?" The auctioneer's eyes quickly survey the room as his assistants strain to leave no bidder unnoticed.

Suddenly, he shouts:

"New bidder in the back of the room at 5 million dollars!"

Heads turn to see who has entered the fray. The emergence of a new bidder adds validation to each buyer's belief in the wisdom of

> Note how many people bid low. They help get the whole process going.

> The opening bids are way under the likely valuation range.

> The presence of many buyers discourages bargain hunting.

bidding. The intensity of bidding that has now emerged, unleashes an additional emotion not related to value. It is the urge to be the victor and stand out amongst others. It now translates into elevated arms and waving paddles. What a sight!

> Each bid validates the wisdom of the last buyer's bid.

"Do I have five and a half million?"

"Yes!" he yells. *"Thank you, Madam."*

Hearts skip a beat, heads strain, gasps continue as the bidding goes up and up. With the presence of so many buyers, no one is worried about overpaying.

> Winning can soon replace price as a prime consideration.

"Do I have six million? Yes, to the right. Do I hear six and a half? Yes, thank you, sir," he says, smiling kindly into the eyes of the latest bidder.

"We have six and a half million dollars. Do I hear seven million?"

> The presence of multiple buyers dispels fear of over-paying.

Winning is now everything. As the great philosopher Thomas Hobbes (1588-1679) said, at such moments the thoughts "are to the desires as scouts and spies, to range abroad and find the way to the things desired."[1]

> Valuation is important, but the presence of multiple bidders easily rules the day.

The power that comes from having money now rules. With bids rising above the valuation range, all the exhaustive research into pricing and cataloging to create a defensible value is superseded by a frenzy of buyers focused on winning. Valuations initially serve to establish comfort, but now it is the auctioneer's skill at orchestrating the process that will create or add value. Price is now a function of marketing.

The new bidder in the back of the room raises his paddle and nods to seven million dollars.

"*We have seven million dollars!*" shouts the auctioneer excitedly. "*Do I have seven and a half million?*"

The audience pauses. Heads turn left and right. Eyes then dart around the room searching for who will bid up next.

"*I have seven million dollars in the back of the room. Do I hear seven and a half million?*" he repeats.

Silence, fidgeting, strained necks, heads popping up like submarine periscopes.

"*Last Call. I have seven million dollars. Going once, going...*"

Suddenly, near the front a paddle rises tentatively.

"*Thank you, Madam! We have seven and a half million dollars, ladies and gentlemen. Do I have eight?*"

The paddle in the back of the room slowly rises with the buyer's nod of acquiescence.

"*I have eight million dollars. Do I have eight and a half million?*" The lady up front cautiously raises her paddle yet again.

"*I have eight and a half million dollars from the lady at the front. Do I have nine million dollars? Nine million dollars?*" he asks again. "*Do I have a bid for nine million dollars?*"

The paddle at the back rises.

"*Ladies and gentlemen, I have nine million dollars at the back of the room. Do I hear nine and a half million?*"

> Price is a function of marketing, not valuations.

> Note the power of making the Last Call.

> The Last Call induced a higher bid.

> An extra $2M was realized by making the Last Call, almost 30% more.

He smiles at the lady toward the front. She stares at the object, pauses and moves her head left and right.

Sensing exhaustion, but pleased that his Last Call has unleashed two million more dollars of value in less than half a minute, the auctioneer quickly does a scan of the scene and says to all:

"I have nine million dollars. Last Call. All bids in. I have nine million dollars. Going once, going twice. SOLD to the gentlemen in the rear for nine million dollars."

An explosion of applause fortifies the buyer's conviction. Satisfaction is in the air.

> It is important to notice that the Last Call was made twice.
>
> Buyers applaud even though they lost because they feel they lost fairly to the highest bidder.

****

The auction process crystallizes the hope of every luxury seller: buyers freed from hesitancy, willing to act, eager to pay. As you read, keep this auction scene in your mind; we will refer back to it throughout the book. To get the highest price, you and your agent must have this auction mindset guiding your *power marketing* actions; you will need an agent who can harness and master the auctioneer's ability to create fearless and eager buyers.

Let's review the *power marketing* techniques that result in the auction mindset needed to get the highest price.

Specialization

Almost without question the auction house never proceeds without employing a specialist. This is either someone in house or someone outside the auction firm who specializes in this particular market. In addition, they reference catalogues and books that experts may have written about the object. The specialization can be extreme. The smaller the market for an object, the more specialized is the expert consulted.

Value bands for pricing

Long before auction day, the seller of an object takes it to the auction house to be analyzed, researched, and valued. This process is like a homeowner asking an agent for a consultation and valuation.

The auction house's valuers do not provide a valuation until they have thoroughly inspected and analyzed the object—just as your real estate agent must come to know and understand your property, then research replacement value, land value, past sales, as well as properties currently available, all to produce a comparable market analysis ("CMA").

Once the object has been fully researched and documented with all data, including adjustments for rarity or celebrity value and comparable offerings, the auction house will determine its condition and adjust the base price up or down to create a value band of pricing. We suggest that this value band of pricing is exactly what you should expect from your real estate agent. You should be leery of any agent who gives you a fixed price and tells you "this is the value."

Why?

The auction house doesn't know the price that the item will fetch and neither does your agent. In the case of the auction house, if few people come to the auction, the price will be low. If many people fill the room, the price will likely be higher. Therefore, the

> Filling the room and orchestrating the psychology of the sale is what gets the highest price.

auction house provides an estimated range of value, albeit diligently researched and printed in the program. Value is determined by markets, marketing and marketers, not by valuers or appraisers (though valuation is critical to establishing interest and luring buyers - see

Chapter 4). So, too, the value of your luxury home will be determined by the quality of the marketing you choose and your agent provides, sprinkled occasionally with a little good luck, just as in any auction.

Fill the room

Next, in order to fill the room with potential bidders, the auction house will suggest an appropriate marketing plan. This typically includes creating a brochure and publishing the background or provenance of the object. The auction house will target-market known contacts and advertise to unknown buyers. If the object has celebrity or rarity value, the auction house may conduct a publicity campaign. All these marketing steps have one goal: to get as many qualified bidders as possible into the room or on the phone the day of the auction. If they are successful in filling the room, they will get a higher price. If not, they will get less.

Obstructions to bidding removed in advance

Something else should be noted in the auction because it is relatively foreign to real estate sales: obstructions to bidding are removed in advance. For instance, in a real estate transaction title is not researched until after a deal is struck. But in the auction title is researched and guaranteed in advance. This means there is no "out" in the contract or delay to closing. Second, in the auction there is no bidding "subject to getting an appraisal" as in real estate. This means there is no appraisal contingency that could sink the deal. Rather, value is set by the auction. Finally, there is no additional inspection of the object and no contingency for such an inspection. You inspect it in advance and then submit your offer based upon that inspection.

In this way, at least three contingencies to bidding are removed and cannot stand in the way of doing a deal. There is no reason that similar obstructions to completing a deal in real estate cannot be removed in advance.

Sole buyer syndrome

Sometimes in the real estate sales process homeowners will say to their agent: *"You only have to find that one buyer in a million."* But what if only one buyer shows up in the auction room? Put yourself in that position. As you sit there, alone in a sea of empty chairs, what are you thinking?

> The more people who want something, the greater is its perceived worth.

We call this situation "sole buyer syndrome." As a buyer wouldn't you wonder why no one else showed up? Wouldn't you be nervous because others are not present to validate your good sense and judgment? Without that validation, you are not likely to bid aggressively for the object. After all, the more people who want something, the greater is its perceived worth.

Comfort from another's desire

Recall what happens on a typical auction day. The room is packed with buyers. The atmosphere is abuzz with anticipation. As the starting draws near, attendees' interest in the acquisition increases with the number of people coming into the room. The more who want this object, the greater their comfort to bid, the higher the selling price

Fear of loss

It is also true that the more buyers who want something, the greater is the fear of losing it, and the greater that fear, the more buyers will pay for it. Thus, the fear of loss must be ever-present in the marketing process and it is your agent's job to keep it there. Your agent can accomplish this best by making interest in the property known to all other buyers (and their agents). That is precisely why the auctioneer begins the bidding process with low offers. The auctioneer wants to demonstrate just how many people want the object being sold. That large number of initial raised hands serves to insert the fear of loss early in the bidding process.

A low starting price also raises comfort

By starting the bidding low and getting as many hands as possible raised at the start, those many raised hands help the auctioneer to keep the fear of loss ever-present, while also increasing everyone's comfort to bid. Unlike the real estate process where the agent begins by telling potential buyers the highest price, i.e. the asking price, the auctioneer begins with many low opening bids which verify that many want this property. Those low bids get everyone comfortable with the thought of bidding. The greater the number of raised hands, the greater the comfort each buyer has in their individual decision to bid. Equally important, the more powerful is the validation of their wisdom and good taste in bidding. Moreover, the presence of these many buyers induced by the auctioneer's openness to low initial bids releases additional desire for the object. This desire is what really sets the value because, as we said earlier, the more buyers who want something, the greater is its perceived worth.

Moving the audience up in price

Next, the auctioneer must make a quick judgment call as to the size of the increments for raising the bidding. The increments must be small enough to retain the existing bidders and bring in new buyers. Bidders always believe that just one more small bid higher will secure them the prize.

> In real estate we usually start asking prices high and work down with a series of seller price cuts.

In contrast to the auctioneer who starts the bidding low and builds momentum, in real estate we usually start high, then with a series of seller price cuts, we work down to where some momentum can build.

The public nature

Note that an auction is usually a public bidding process. In stark contrast, the real estate bidding process is intentionally concealed. At auction everyone involved has the ability to see the buyers raise their hands and voice their bids. Unlike in real estate, the auction process does not shy away from the public aspect. Rather it encourages it. As you will see, we encourage agents to make the real estate marketing and selling process less secret and more open.

The heat of the auction

As the bidding continues, the auctioneer makes a judgment as to how much is left in the bidders' pockets and how much more can be extracted from their hopes. This expertise is one of the reasons why the seller hired the auctioneer.

Late bidders are sometimes new bidders and they enliven the auction. They may have intended to bid initially, but before stepping in they waited to gauge competition and see how high bids would go. These late entrants not only wait to see how much competition is present, but they want to be assured that there actually is competition. You will see this dramatically played out in the last pages of this book.

When these late entrants start bidding, the auctioneer shouts "New Bidder!" He wants everyone to feel momentum is increasing, not dissipating. He knows that new entrants re-enforce the threat of multiple, simultaneous bidders, and he knows that it is this threat that will get the highest price. This kind of orchestration is the heart of *power marketing.*

The Last Call

The auctioneer's most important final marketing technique is to make the Last Call. Just as the auction reaches its emotional apex, he threatens to close down the process, yet gives everyone one more chance to bid higher. Because of the transparency of the process and the opportunity to make a last bid, the buyers feel comfortable with the rules. As a result, the auction reignites. Suddenly, in our example an additional two million dollars of value is unleashed.

By the end of the auction, the auctioneer has conducted a symphony of orchestrated emotions and positive feelings. The buyer feels good about the fairness of the process and most importantly, about winning. The seller is satisfied to have gotten the highest price the market can bear.

The Takeaway

The auction provides an outstanding example of *power marketing* concepts:

- *Specialization* is *de rigueur* for all auction houses and most consumers would hardly think of dealing with any that don't specialize in the object being sold.

- *Auction houses never set prices:* Auction houses just provide reasonable and thoughtful guesses as to the likely range within which an object may sell.

- *Price is a function of marketing*: Price is not determined by homeowners, valuers, or real estate agents, but by the market that has been created. That market is determined by the number of people who want the property and the marketer's skill at orchestrating their desire.

- *The goal of power marketing* is to induce competition within this market by getting multiple bidders vying simultaneously.

- *Comfort releases value*: The more comfortable buyers become, the more value is unleashed.

- *Three obstructions to bidding are removed in advance*: (1) title is provided to the buyer or guaranteed, (2) an appraisal or valuation is done and available to all, (3) inspection of the object is complete and buyers are satisfied as to condition.

- *Fill the room:* Initial marketing does not focus on "finding one buyer in a million," but rather on "filling the room" with as many buyers as possible, even if that means encouraging low offers. Everything possible is done to avoid "sole buyer syndrome."

- *Awareness:* The presence of other buyers is intentionally disclosed. Such awareness validates desire, raises comfort, lessens the fear of bidding, and generates a sense of openness and fairness about the overall process.

- *Validating belief and desire*: Low offers are important because they are plentiful and the multiplicity of buyer interest validates other buyer's desire and belief in the wisdom of bidding, liberating each bidder emotionally and psychologically to pay more.

- *Winning*: The desire to win among competitive, successful and wealthy buyers can become everything, sometimes even surpassing value considerations.

- *The Last Call*: Making the Last Call can add 5% to 30% more to the final price.

- *True value:* The competition unleashed by *power marketing* determines the true value of a property, which can be below or above the listed price.

Key differences between selling through the real estate process versus the luxury auction process

	Luxury Auction	Real Estate
Goal	Highest price	Get close to ask
Appraisal	Done before	Done after
Inspection	Done before	Done after
Title Search	Done before	Done after
Expertise	Specialized	General
Price	Starts low	Starts high
Price	Set by auction	Set as ask
Process	Open	Usually veiled
Buyer comfort	From others' bids	From a bargain
Value	From competition	Must defend
Last Call	Required	Rare

Chapter 2:
Challenges to reaching your goal

Challenge # 1: The market for your property is extremely small

Why should you worry about "filling the room?" After all, if you put your property on the Multiple Listing Service, won't the buyers come?

The answer to this question is "no" for several reasons. Most importantly, the market for a luxury property is small, very small. In fact, it is so small that when charted the market is barely visible, as you will see. In addition, the few buyers out there may not be in the market when you are ready to sell. To understand why it is so small, we have to first define "luxury real estate."

The "million dollar and up" definition

Once upon a time luxury real estate had a clear definition: It consisted of properties valued at more than a million dollars. Even today our culture tends to think luxury is "million dollar and up." Therefore, let's start by asking: How big is the market based upon the "million dollar and up" definition? There have been two prior attempts to determine its size (1) by the Census Bureau and (2) by the Federal Reserve in its Survey of Consumer Finances.

Based upon the 2000 census, the Census Bureau concluded that there were 313,759 single-family, million-dollar homes in the country.[2] Unfortunately, the Census underestimated the market by limiting itself to single-family homes; it did not, for instance, include the tens of thousands of million-dollar-plus condominiums and cooperatives in high-end areas. Also, the 2000 Census counted only primary residences, leaving out the many second and even third or fourth million-dollar homes. Finally, the Census data excluded any town with fewer than 100,000 people. As a result, it omitted Beverly Hills, Palm Beach, Greenwich, Gross Pointe, and the innumerable other small enclaves of wealth that form the backbone of the luxury real estate market. Because of this undercounting, the 313,759 figure is too low.

A second attempt was made by the Survey of Consumer Finances (SCF) in 2001. It reported that there were about 850,000 households in the United States that owned primary residences worth at least a million dollars.[3] This conclusion was based upon an extrapolation from a very small sample, resulting in a figure nearly three times that determined by the Census and a differential of 536,241. The resulting huge discrepancy has led the Joint Center of Housing Studies at Harvard University to conclude: "Exactly where the actual number of 'million dollar' homes owned as primary residences lies between these estimates [and] is impossible to calculate."[4]

The "million dollar and up" market as a percentage of the whole

While it may be impossible to precisely calculate, still the above studies give us a good sense of how small the "million dollar and up" market is in relation to the whole. For example, if we were to take the approximately 313,000 single-family homes the 2000 Census claims are million dollar and up and divide this number by the fifty-five million single family homes that existed then, the market is 0.6 of 1 percent of the whole.

If we consider the SCF's claim of 850,000 million-dollar homes and divide that number by the 70,000,000 owner-occupied housing units, we still get a small percentage figure—just 1.21 percent of all homes.[5]

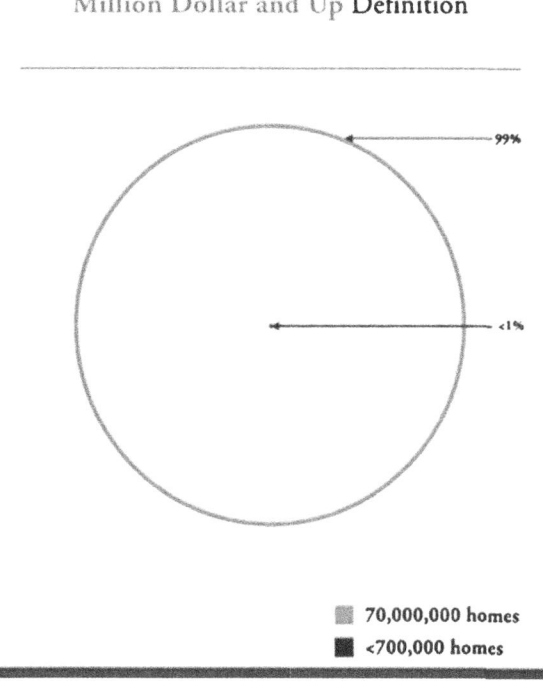

Estimated Luxury Market Using the Million Dollar and Up Definition

- 70,000,000 homes
- <700,000 homes

From this, we can at least conclude that in 2000-2001 the number of U.S. million dollar homes ranged somewhere between 0.6 percent and 1.21 percent of the total of all owner-occupied housing units.

We agree with Harvard that the truth lies between these estimates. Believing one figure is too low and the other is too high, why not just average the two? We can then reasonably determine that the "million dollar and up" portion consists of 0.9 of 1 percent of the market. Going forward we will simply say that it consists of "less than 1 percent" of the whole US housing market.

Having quantified it enough for our purposes here, the "million dollar and up" definition still begs the question about markets like Marin and Sonoma Counties in California; or Palm Beach and Beverly Hills; or Manhattan or Greenwich (where almost 70 percent of all sales in 2012 were over one million and more than 43% were over two million). In Palm Beach and Beverly Hills, a million dollars will probably not even buy a building lot, let alone a luxury property. Million-dollar homes in these markets are as ordinary as ranch houses in a 1950's subdivision. Thus, the million dollar and up definition defines a product that is no longer considered luxurious in the very areas that form the core of the luxury housing market.

The 10 percent definition

The other common definition of "luxury real estate" today does not provide any help and actually makes matters worse. It defines luxury real estate as "the top 10 percent of any market." This is the definition largely used by the real estate brokerage industry and has a very democratic quality to it. It allows for every market in the country to have a piece of luxury real estate, whether it is a $240,000 home in a $125,000 average market or a $5M home where the average is $2M. This definition allows the brokerage industry to call the top end of every market the luxury market, whether the properties comprising it are luxurious or not.

This definition has another major flaw. If, as the Census says, the U.S. has fifty-five million single family owner-occupied homes, or as the SCF says, the U.S. has seventy million owner-occupied housing units, then by looking through the lens of the top 10 percent definition, five to seven million homes make up the "luxury real estate" market. Suddenly, the top 10 percent definition has increased the highest government estimate of 850,000 by *nine times*. As a result, the top 10% definition defines the class so expansively that it overestimates "luxury real estate" to the point of trivializing it.

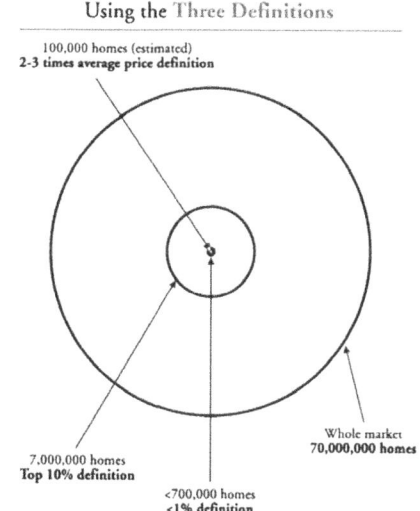

Toward a new definition

Because the two most widely used definitions are so deeply flawed, here we define a luxury property as one that is "2-3 x the average price" of all homes in a particular geographic market and has certain "requisite qualities."

Our definition offers the same flexibility as the top 10 percent model. It, too, accounts for fluctuations in various markets. But unlike the top 10 percent model, some markets, based upon this starting point, will not have any luxury real estate at all. This is fine. For a more granular discussion of our "2-3 times average price + requisite qualities" definition, see Appendix 1.

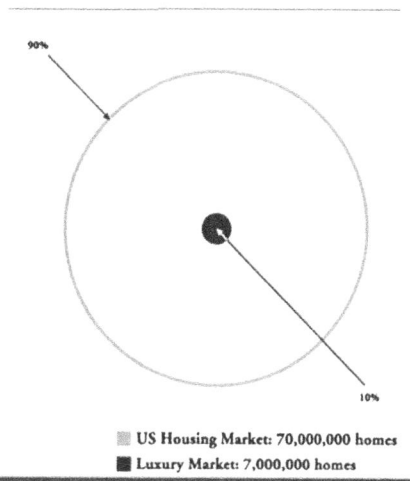

Even smaller than we have articulated

Whether we use the "million dollar and up" definition that indicates "less than 1%" of homes are luxury or our much more restrictive "2-3 times average price + requisite qualities" definition, the market is extremely small. But, in reality it is actually about 20 times smaller or about 1/20th that number. Why? Because not all of these owners are in the market to buy at one time.

> For example, about 5-6 % of American homeowners move yearly, and therefore only 5-6% of the estimated 700,000 "million dollar and up" homeowners, or about thirty thousand to forty thousand are in the market in any one year.
>
> Using our narrower "2-3 times average price + requisite qualities" definition, we estimate that our definition reduces it even further by at least a factor of 5 to a market made up of only about six to eight thousand buyers annually. [6]

Thus, whether you average the Census and SCF data to get 1/20 of "less than 1 percent" for the "million dollar and up market" or you follow our more restrictive "2-3 x average price + requisite qualities" definition, the primary difference of the luxury market is its tiny size. The target market is extraordinarily small.

The mistakes it leads to

Overestimating the size of the luxury real estate market may lead you and your agent to underestimate the time and skill required to access it. Overestimating its size leads to imagining greater liquidity than actually exists and results in mistakes in pricing (often overpricing). Overstating the size and liquidity also leads to confusion about the expected time on market. Perhaps most seriously, it gives the impression that any agent is qualified to operate within the luxury market and obscures the need for a different marketing mindset with which to market, reach, and handle the target buyers, i.e. *power marketing*.

Committing any one of these mistakes can cost you considerably and, based on our 2-3 times definition, could cost you hundreds of thousands if not millions of dollars.

Challenge # 2: The luxury real estate market is highly illiquid

Not only is the luxury market small, but it often lacks the liquidity expected from markets in the United States. Moves in the luxury market, up and down, can occur with a herd instinct and with little notice. This is because you and those in your social group are largely invested in the same stock markets, often through the same bank trust departments, mutual funds and money managers. When your wealth declines or rises, it does so along with that of your friends. This gives the luxury market wild swings in liquidity. Unit sales can easily drop by 50 to 80 percent even when the overall market might be experiencing only a 10 to 20 percent drop.

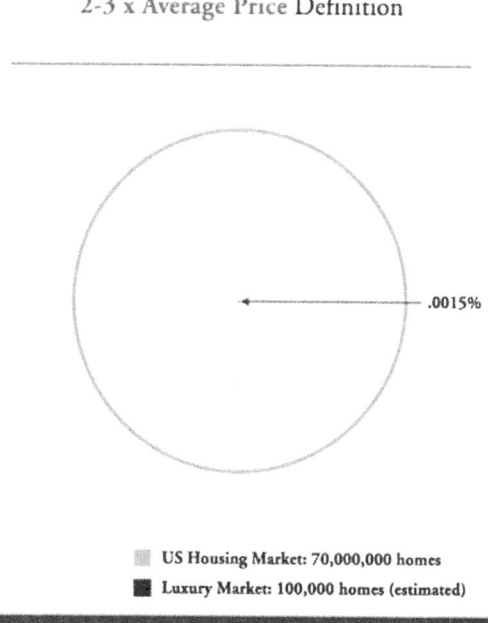

Estimated Luxury Market Using the
2-3 x Average Price Definition

US Housing Market: 70,000,000 homes
Luxury Market: 100,000 homes (estimated)

As an example, during the 1990-1991 recession, we sat in our offices with paltry buyer response to a slew of different marketing efforts. Week after week agents provided field reports of no showings for our listings. The few offers came from bargain seekers who provided sometimes bizarre terms (we once had an offer of twenty gallons of prized bull sperm on a two million dollar house). During such recessions, everyone feels poor and seems to withdraw from the market.

A more recent example of this occurred in early 2009 when a report that focuses on the five million dollar and up luxury coop market in Manhattan, wrote: *"...it is not possible to determine the price declines in this [$5M and up] sector because there is simply not enough empirical data to suggest a pattern."* [7] As a result, the firm compiling the data looked to the market under $5M where it said, *"There have been enough transactions to determine that this market has seen prices decrease 15 to 20 percent."* Note that even in this "more liquid" market, they had to give an estimated range for the price changes instead of real figures. Not surprisingly, that summer they found the market so slow they suspended their luxury market report for that period altogether.[8]

Of course, we all know that wealth did not disappear in either 1991 or 2008-2009. What disappeared *en masse* was confidence. Those who still had money found themselves frozen into doing nothing until the economic outlook cleared. Liquidity evaporated and took confidence with it.

Challenge # 3: Pricing luxury real estate is more difficult, volatile and far less precise.

You have probably spent considerable sums creating a truly distinctive property. It was probably designed to be unique and not comparable to other properties in the market. You may even resent anyone (including your agent) trying to compare it to other properties.

You are probably correct. Your property is incomparable and because of that, it is much more difficult to price. Luxury markets are composed of unique homes that offer fewer market comparisons. The result is that pricing luxury homes is much more difficult, far less precise and more of an art than a science.

Challenge # 4: As a luxury seller, you are highly sophisticated, a great negotiator and very smart.

As a seller of luxury real estate, you represent the most sophisticated consumer in the real estate market. You may be the chairman, CEO, CFO, founder or largest investor in one or more companies. You may be a celebrity or have enjoyed your lifestyle for generations. In any case, you are smart, good at negotiating and are accustomed to dealing with the best in the business world. You expect results, good management and accountability. You probably are not accustomed to being managed. Thus, you may want to micro-manage the whole process. Finding an agent with skills even remotely similar to yours, may be exceedingly difficult.

We have written this book so you can understand the sophisticated marketing principles necessary for an agent to get you the highest price and you will find resources to help in locating the right agent at both the front and the back. You may also find those skills in the agent who gave you this book.

> Buyers can afford your property because they earned their money making wise decisions, not making mistakes like overpaying for a home.

Challenge # 5: Luxury buyers are just as smart as sellers.

Occasionally, a seller/client wants to hire us with the hope that we can pull the wool over a buyer's eyes and get someone foolishly to overpay for their property. In particular, sellers in the luxury market are most curious about international buyers, hoping that we can find a sheikh or foreign magnate to overpay for their home. If you share this point of view, know that multimillion-dollar buyers can afford your property because they earned their money making wise decisions, not making mistakes like overpaying for a home.

Remember this phrase: "In luxury real estate, buyers are just as smart as sellers." All the advice we provide is based upon an enormous respect for the intelligence of luxury buyers. Because of this respect, in Chapter 4 we will provide a different way to start pricing in order to determine a credible, defensible and saleable asking price. We will also show you how to create a selling sound-bite that the smart luxury buyer will want to hear and to which he or she will likely respond. Read on.

The buyer's advisers

While unaware or uninformed luxury buyers are rare, even if you find one, he or she will almost always have a slew of lawyers, accountants, bankers, or other trusted financial advisers around to ensure they do not overpay for anything. This sophisticated committee of professionals is in place to prevent a buyer from making a buying mistake.

Finally, even if the buyer does not have a committee of advisers, they have a Buyer Agent. The real estate industry changed radically around 1990 with the introduction of buyer agency. Now, buyers hire agents to represent them and that agent's key fiduciary duty is for the buyer not to overpay. If occasionally the buyer is not as smart as the seller, their agent may be.

Challenge # 6: The luxury market is characterized by sellers who do not have to sell and buyers who do not have to buy. This creates a lack of urgency to act on the part of all.

John Maynard Keynes (1883-1946) wrote that markets can remain irrational longer than we can remain solvent. One of the perks of being rich is that you have staying power to withstand market declines. You probably have more than one home and many different sources of equity. Often your homes are not leveraged, but paid for in cash; thus, you have no financial urgency to act. Or, if you have to raise cash, you have more liquid assets to sell before you entertain low-ball offers on your home.

Buyers who do not have to buy

In the same vein, buyers of multimillion dollar homes do not have to buy. Like you, they can wait. For them, buying is more a lifestyle choice than a necessity, so a purchase does not have to happen today or tomorrow or next month. Luxury buyers move on their own timetable.

A "market" lacking an urgency to act is the key characteristic of luxury real estate and requires special *power marketing* tactics to break the stalemate.

Challenge # 7: Focus and specialization

The final obstacle to getting the highest price is the generalist nature of most real estate agents. What you need is (1) an agent who specializes in the upper tier, (2) demonstrates expertise in *listing* and marketing properties (vs. just working with buyers), (3) has access to the data you need to price and sell your home, and (4) knows *power marketing* techniques and strategies.

Some of the most powerful words an agent can say to you in a listing presentation are *"I specialize in what you own"* or *"I specialize in listing luxury properties."* When they do, you have a compelling reason to consider them and perhaps a good reason to hire them.

The Takeaway

- Challenge # 1: The "luxury real estate" market is very small. To understand it, we have to define "luxury real estate."

- "Million dollar-and-up" defines it as "less than 1 percent" of the entire housing market.

- Nonetheless, the "million dollar-and-up" definition has been superseded in many prime luxury markets where million dollar sales are quite ordinary.

- A better solution for defining luxury real estate is "2-3 x the average price + requisite qualities" which admittedly narrows the definition of luxury real estate even more.

- Whatever definition you use, the actual market is about 1/20th the size because only about 1/20th of the potential buyers are in the market during any one year.

- Challenge # 2: The market is highly illiquid.

- Challenge # 3: Pricing "incomparable" properties is much more difficult than simply using comparables and requires a different starting point (see Chapter 4).

- Challenge # 4: Sellers are more sophisticated and expect an agent to match their skills.

- Challenge # 5: Luxury real estate buyers are just as sophisticated and smart as luxury sellers and, therefore, all marketing to them must begin with enormous respect for their intelligence.

- Challenge # 6: The luxury market is characterized by sellers who do not have to sell and buyers who do not have to buy, creating a lack of urgency to act.

- Challenge # 7: To overcome the generalist nature of most agents, you need a *power marketer.*

Chapter 3:
The *power* *marketing* solution

A *power marketer* thinks as follows:

Power marketing Mindset #1: The small size and lack of liquidity in the luxury market requires that competition be created by finding two or more buyers.

Recently, we saw an ad in the *New York Times* that summarized perfectly what is needed to overcome the challenges of the small luxury market and its lack of liquidity. The ad was from the telephone carrier, Sprint. The words are theirs, but the sentiments are at the heart of *power marketing*:

"Competition is everything. Competition is the steady hand at our back, pushing us to faster, better, smarter, simpler, lighter, thinner, *cooler. Competition is American. Competition plays fair...Competition has many friends, but its very best is the consumer. Competition has many believers and we are among them."*

Throughout the marketing of your home, whatever you and your agent do must have as its central goal the creation of competition. By writing this book we are even providing competition for your real estate agent. How? By empowering and arming you with an understanding of *power marketing*, your knowledge provides the competitive catalyst for agents to improve their marketing skill and in doing so, that of the entire real estate brokerage business. Now, not just a quality agent knows what to do, but you, the luxury consumer, know, too. Two people knowing what to do is better than one (or none). By improving both your and your agent's skill set, competition allows you both to win.

By empowering you with knowing how to get the highest price, not only are we trying to improve the real estate brokerage industry by making it more competitive (and at the same time, heighten its value), but earlier we indicated that your agent must create a competitive market for your property by finding not one, but two or more buyers. Let us explain.

Many years ago a notable luxury marketing firm claimed that its mission was "to find that one buyer in a million." We always liked that slogan. It set the firm apart by projecting a certain exclusivity. Finding one buyer in a million is also what many a luxury seller articulates as their agent's job. Over and over we have heard the phrase "you only have to find that one buyer."

That said, what would happen if your agent found only one buyer? Would one buyer bid up for your property? Or would that sole buyer prefer to use her "one in a million" status to negotiate a lower price? A single buyer, in fact, puts you in a weak position because one buyer does not a market make. Finding only one buyer empowers that buyer and puts you at a disadvantage. That buyer dictates the psychology, the negotiations, the terms, and ultimately the price paid for your home. Finding "one buyer in a million" is actually the opposite of what you want. It is also the opposite of *power marketing*.

Only by finding two or more buyers and introducing competition can you compel the sales process toward a successful conclusion. Without the market created by such competition, buyers have in effect a monopoly on your property and will do exactly what any self-interested person would do: bid low, if at all. Finding two or more buyers is imperative, but also markedly more difficult, due to the small size and lack of liquidity in the luxury market. Nonetheless, your agent's mindset must focus on doing just that.

Markets and creating them

While it would be wonderful to assume your agent is adept at creating markets, the reality is that most agents are not. For this you can blame success. The reason is that over the last one hundred years, the National Association of Realtors® (together with hundreds of state and local boards of Realtors) has created Multiple Listing Services (MLS's) in virtually every market in America. These MLS's are based on "universal offers of cooperation and compensation" between and among agents under which fees are shared.

As a result, the organized real estate brokerage profession has done a superb job of creating a market for most U.S. real estate through the MLS. The U.S. market is liquid and efficient, transparent, accessible and highly cost effective. It provides quality guidance on what a similar property has sold for in the past and therefore what it might sell for in the future. Because of the efficiency that exists in the U.S. market, most agents rarely concern themselves with creating a competitive market for their listings.

However, the MLS's efficiency wilts for luxury real estate. Not only is the market small, but the few buyers may not even be looking in the market, nor have hired an agent or know they want your property. They may be off in the south of France for several weeks or they may be at their second or third home. They could be in the middle of a major corporate takeover or just not be interested in looking when you are ready to sell. Often they are interested only if a property comes on in a particular location or with certain amenities or features. Thus, they don't even know they are buyers until presented with a property. As a result, for the most expensive and unique properties, you need a mindset that uses the MLS and the many other tools we review in Chapter 7 to orchestrate the creation of a market for your home. Doing that requires a *power marketing* mindset.

Power marketing Mindset # 2: The *threat* of competition can sometimes be just as effective as actual competition.

While finding two or more buyers to create competition must always be a *power marketer's* goal, sometimes it may not be necessary. Rather the *threat* of finding two or more buyers can often provide the competition needed to prompt a successful initial bid or even result in a successful sale (see Chapter 13). From where can such threats come?

A good agent's reputation for success can be a threat.

A successful real estate listing agent can be a powerful threat to buyers. Why? Because knowing that a property is listed with such an agent gives a good indication that properties listed by them are likely to be sold. This can eventually prompt hesitant buyers to make an offer. For example, in talking with potential buyers, we always mention our 93% track record of success while expressing our confidence that the property in question—like other properties we have listed—will also be sold. Often, simply the threat of unleashing a *power marketer's* skill is enough to move a buyer to bid or to raise their bid.

The threat from knowing of other buyers

A threat can also come from a buyer's awareness of other buyers. For example, a buyer may see other buyers at open houses or during orchestrated, sequential showings (see Mindset # 5). A threat can also come from an agent's aggressive or thoughtful national and international marketing campaign. Remember, orchestrating a threat can be as powerful as having an actual second or third buyer.

Why your first offer is often your best

The value of a threat allows us to understand the old adage: "your first offer is often your best offer." The threat of not knowing how many buyers are interested in a property often moves first bidders to bid fast and bid high. This threat is only present for the first few days or weeks of a listing because only at that time is a buyer pained by the insecurity of not yet knowing the results of an agent's marketing efforts. During this initial period of uncertainty, bidders often make their best offer. But if there are no offers by the third or fourth week, the threat begins to dissipate and buyers stop thinking about aggressive bidding.

Pricing provides a competitive threat, too

While we will deal extensively with pricing in the next chapter, here we want to mention a pricing strategy that is guaranteed to unleash the *threat* of often fierce competition. It is, however, also a strategy most luxury homeowners are uncomfortable in following.

> …you may want your property to be listed above the market and your pricing be as different as you perceive your property to be.

For years, great real estate coaches and trainers have advised their agent-customers that the most effective way to sell real estate is to price properties close to or even below market value. This, they correctly argue, is how to release competition and create a market for a property.

Based on this advice, if you really want to *power market* your property, just list it under or at the low end of your valuation range and you will unleash a torrent of competitive demand. This is like the auctioneer starting the bidding low and then orchestrating the process higher. By listing the property low and hiring a *power marketer* to orchestrate the buyers up in price, it will sell, and with the right *power marketing* orchestration, it may even sell above the valuation range. Why? Bargains themselves unleash competition. When trainers and coaches teach that such value pricing sells real estate, they are really teaching that pricing can be the spark that ignites competition and creates markets. In effect, they teach that the power in *power marketing* can come from value pricing.

But we also know that as a luxury homeowner, only rarely will you risk pricing your property at the low end of the valuation range. You fear under-pricing and leaving money on the table. Your fears also may emanate from a lack of confidence in your agent's *power marketing* expertise. As a result, you may want your property to be listed above the market and your pricing to be as different as you perceive your property to be. This often means that it gets priced outside the valuation range. Understanding this, we will help you in the next chapter by introducing a concept called Core Value Pricing. We will show you how to price and present your property with credible, defensible and clearly demonstrable value, but in a way that provides savvy luxury buyers with a discount to your property's Core Value which, in turn, will help to raise comfort and generate the threat of competition. Don't miss "Seven Step Pricing" in Chapter 4.

Power marketing Mindset #3: The price or value of your real estate is not fixed, but should be understood as oscillating within a band of possible prices.

You should never think that your property is going to sell at a certain price. Prices move up and down weekly, daily and hourly. A property valued on April 1 may face entirely new market conditions by the time a buyer makes an offer. By June 1 the stock market may have crashed (or spiked), a war may have started or some other event may materially affect the price you will get. Because no one can predict the future, price expectations must adjust to the changing tides. Thus, value will change with many variables:

- Market conditions

- The number of buyers found or the threat that can be created

- The value you have demonstrated to the buyer

- The comfort level of the buyers (usually based upon the number of other buyers)

- How well your agent has *power marketed* the orchestration of the sale

As a seller you may consciously or unconsciously recognize that markets fluctuate and prices are not fixed. But you usually use this insight to justify adding a "little more" to the asking price by indicating that you "need a little negotiating room." Often this can put you above the defensible value your agent suggests. Your agent may feel frustrated by this request because they may have already included "a little extra" in their Comparable Market Analysis ("CMA") or Broker Price Opinion ("BPO"). If you both increase the price, your joint action may price the property indefensibly high, discouraging buyers and other agents or worse, resulting in the listing being dead on arrival.

A lot of time and effort should go into determining a credible, defensible asking price, but know that it will be nothing more than a well thought out educated guess. In the end, you don't control prices; only the market does. What you can influence is the marketing which ultimately creates the market that sets the price.

Because markets are dynamic and change constantly, you must confine your selling expectations to a reasonable valuation band, not to a fixed asking price. Then you must realize that just like in the auction, it is marketing and the orchestration of competitive bidders that will get you the highest price within this valuation band.

Power marketing Mindset #4: Power marketers seek to orchestrate multiple bidders or the threat thereof to act *simultaneously*

While this principal has been implicit in everything we have said thus far, it is important enough to emphasize explicitly: *you must have two or more buyers or the threat thereof, bidding on a property <u>simultaneously</u> in order to get the sophisticated buyer to act.* If someone bids in May and someone else bids in July, it doesn't have the necessary impact on the bidding process as when they bid simultaneously.

As we saw in Chapter 1, the momentum generated in the auction from simultaneous bidding is so enticing and contagious, that buyers who might be hesitant to act can be swept up in the enthusiasm of the sale. This only works, however, if your agent, like the auctioneer, has everyone in the same room bidding together at the same time.

Power marketing Mindset #5: *Power marketers* control the psychology of the sale with fear of loss and do everything possible to raise buyer comfort

In order to control the psychology of the sale, one of the core skills at which your agent must be adept is orchestrating the following two emotions.

Fear of loss

Fear of loss exists when there is a perceived threat, as in the beginning of the sales process when there is uncertainty about the success of the marketing. The possibility of its success threatens the buyers with loss. It can also emerge when buyers are presented with a tempting bargain that they fear losing out on (recall in the auction that at the outset many buyers bid low hoping for a bargain). It also exists when buyers are aware of each other, either by seeing each other's coming and going at showings or by your agent telling buyer-agents about other buyer interest. The last point requires further elaboration.

Some listing agents keep quiet about multiple interest because they worry about creating an "auction situation." In so doing, they are ignoring the goal of all marketing and as a consequence never reach it. But in addition, discouraging an "auction situation" prevents fear of loss from entering the negotiations. Worse, fearing an "auction situation" can even offend buyers. Let us explain.

In thirty years of owning and managing real estate offices we have seen that the greatest number of complaints come from angry buyers who lost a property because they were never informed that other bidders were in play. They felt cheated by not having the opportunity to bid higher. Either the listing agent or the selling agent or both feared an "auction situation" when, in fact, they should have been aiming to create one. Thus, ironically, when buyers know of the presence of other bidders, it not only helps to create fear of loss, but it also creates a transparency for the process which allows them to feel comfortable that fair play is present.

Your agent, therefore, must keep the fear of loss present by making known the bidding (not the bids) of other buyers, or the threat thereof.

Creating buyer comfort through the presence of others

The second emotion your agent must be skilled at orchestrating is buyer comfort. Ironically, the easiest way for an agent to create such comfort is through the presence (or threat) of other buyers, i.e. competition. The presence (or threat) of other buyers creates the very comfort necessary for a smart, highly sophisticated buyer to bid or to bid higher. Everyone in real estate

> A buyer can be dormant for months, but suddenly when a second buyer comes along and makes an offer, the first buyer scrambles into action.

knows this. The presence of other buyers confirms and validates each buyer's wisdom. Multiple buyers also confirm each other's good taste in location, style, and amenities.

Let us illustrate with one of our own experiences. We listed our resort property with an agent. A buyer saw the property and liked it, and asked if we had any offers. Our agent answered honestly that there had been none. The buyer then asked to be alerted "if anything happened" with the property. Nothing happened for months as we languished during the market meltdown of 2008 to 2009. Then, some four months after the first buyer saw the property, a second buyer made a low ball offer. We needed to sell our property and we asked our listing agent if there was anyone else out there. We were assured that this was the only offer and we should take it. It did not hurt that it came with a 50% down payment and a short financing contingency for the balance. We verbally accepted the low offer.

Our listing agent then conscientiously noted in the MLS that our property had an "Accepted Offer." The alert agent for the first buyer from four months earlier saw the notation in the MLS and called our listing agent, irate that she had not been informed as requested. Immediately, she called her buyer and told her that there was activity on our property and that, in fact, we had accepted an offer. Within a day we were offered 15% more without any financing contingency and with a quick closing.

This story clearly demonstrates the importance of creating buyer comfort through the presence of other buyers. While our agent dropped the ball by not calling the other agent when we had an offer, thanks to a diligent MLS notation, the buyer's comfort was raised, albeit belatedly and accidentally instead of deliberately and by design. Nonetheless, as a consequence we sold the property to that buyer for 19% more than the low ball offer.

> The comfort of having competition allowed the first buyer willingly and gladly to do what she would not do four months earlier.

More recently as this book was going to press, we were handed yet another example of buyers' comfort being raised by competition. Linda listed a $5.65M property here in Greenwich which very quickly resulted in a $4.8M and a $5M offer from a buyer who could have afforded to pay full price. In the course of the negotiations the buyer stopped bidding. He indicated that he (1) wanted to buy the property, and (2) would pay more, but he wanted competition in order to raise his price. Did he really ask for competition? Well, yes and no. He did not explicitly say to bring competition, but he did ask to be kept informed if other buyers were to bid and when they did, (i.e. when he had competition), he would then raise his offer.

Could there be any clearer indication of how a smart, rich buyer who can pay anything, nonetheless, still needs the comfort of knowing that others are bidding? Given the large sums such buyers are spending, perhaps it is even more important that they know others will pay close to what they are thinking of offering. Such buyers do not say outright that they want competition, but in fact that is exactly what is at the heart of their request. It is such competition that validates the wisdom of their choices and gives them added comfort in knowing they are not alone in wanting a property. As a postscript, Linda secured twelve offers on the property. Clearly those many offers created, re-enforced and validated the comfort of all to bid.

Sole buyer syndrome revisited

Let's revisit "sole buyer syndrome." Remember that? It occurs when someone feels he or she is the only buyer for a property. If a buyer is unaware of other interest, the fear of losing the property can morph into the fear that they might actually win it and end up getting something that no one else wants. Thus, if no one is out there validating the wisdom of the buyer's interest, the fear of loss can quickly turn into fear of gain.

You don't want that. You want the fear of loss to be ever present, knowing that it can actually create the comfort necessary to bid. Fear of loss can only come from competition, real or perceived and, ironically, a higher comfort to act comes as a kind of dividend.

Comfort from sequential, orchestrated showings

As we mentioned earlier, one way to allow buyers and their agents to feel the presence of other interest is through orchestrating sequential showings of your property. All this means is setting up appointments near enough to each other that the buyers have time to view the property, but also see someone leaving when they arrive and arriving when they leave. This is not always possible, but your agent should strive to make it so by always trying to cluster showings. You will see this in real life in the telling of the story of Clarendon Court in Chapter 13.

Power marketing Mindset #6: *Power marketing expertise is the primary reason to hire a particular agent over another.*

Many people think all real estate agents are more or less the same. They reason that the only difference among agents is the commission they charge. According to this thinking, you end up with the same result no matter what an agent charges or who they are. For example, while writing this book, we came across a church in our area that was selling a piece of property. To hire an agent the church put out a bidding process and indicated that they did not want to know the name of the agent nor the name of the firm. Instead, all they wanted to know was the commission expected. The church assumed all real estate agents were the same, only what they charged varied.

By now you understand that nothing is farther from the truth. We love the phrase: "Quality is remembered long after price is forgotten." As a successful businessperson, your problem is probably not your ability or even willingness to pay a commission; rather, it is finding a quality agent to hire. That agent needs to know (1) marketing and (2) markets. To help you find agents with marketing expertise, we offer agents the Certified Power Marketer ™ PMpro Designation and will be creating a Directory of such agents who have successfully acquired it. In addition, to help you find agents with market knowledge (versus

PMpro marketing expertise) we have created a Directory of agents who do a Market Report at *http://GetYourHighestPrice/Directory.*

In sum, the *power marketing* agent you hire must recognize that smart, sophisticated luxury buyers do not have to buy and will not do so unless their comfort is raised. It is therefore your agent's job to do so by demonstrating other buyer interest in the property, most notably by creating competition. The willingness to bid and bid higher surfaces when your agent can produce a second or third buyer to bid simultaneously or invokes the threat thereof. In the process, additional buyers always create uncertainty and add to the fear of loss while at the same time paradoxically adding validation to the buyer's choice. That validation raises comfort levels so that buyers can intelligently and comfortably bid up. The skillful orchestration of these two emotions, the fear of loss, and the comfort in not being alone, overcome sole buyer syndrome and position the buyer to bid aggressively, sometimes joyfully and usually eagerly.

Your success in getting the highest price depends on your hiring a *power marketer* who is adept at controlling and orchestrating all such aspects of the psychology of the sale, especially fear of loss and raising buyer comfort through competition. In the next chapter we will show you how to raise the comfort level of buyers to bid even more by doing a Core Value Calculation and then providing a discount to this valuation. Read on.

The Takeaway

- *Power marketing* Mindset #1: The small size and lack of liquidity in the luxury market requires creating competition for your property by finding two or more buyers. We call this creating a market.

- *Power marketing* Mindset #2:   The *threat* of competition can sometimes be just as effective as actual competition.

- *Power marketing* Mindset #3:   The price or value of your real estate is not fixed, but should be understood as oscillating within a *valuation band*.

- *Power marketing* Mindset #4:   *Power marketers* seek to orchestrate multiple bidders, or the threat thereof, to act *simultaneously*.

- *Power marketing* Mindset #5:   your agent's job is to use every means possible to positively control the psychology of the sale.

- *Power marketing* Mindset #6:   Possessing *power marketing* expertise is the primary reason to hire a particular agent. It consists of orchestrating fear of loss while raising comfort levels, especially through knowing of the presence or threat of other buyers.

Chapter 4: Seven Step Pricing - no "fingers in the air"

Now that you have gone to an auction, understand the goal of all marketing and have a *power marketing* mindset, let's price your property. We are going to do so, however, without just sticking a finger in the air and guessing a price for your unique, incomparable luxury home.

Ask yourself the following:

What are the parameters of value within which my property falls?
Its valuation band?
What influences these values?
Where within that valuation band should my property be listed?
How do I arrive at a definitive asking price for the MLS?

How do I not only make the buyer comfortable with my pricing, but actually entice the super smart luxury buyer with the value that my property offers?

Here are the answers.

Step 1. Establish a Core Value Pricing range

Begin pricing by analyzing your property's core or intrinsic value, much as a securities analyst will examine book value as the bedrock value for a security. Just as an investor often likes to buy a stock at a discount to book value, we are going to raise comfort and entice competition by providing a buyer with a discount to what we call Core Value Pricing. Let's begin with how to determine the range of Core Value Pricing.

> We are going to raise comfort and entice competition by providing a buyer with a discount to what we call Core Value.

Core Value Pricing is not much more complicated than understanding the Replacement Value of a property reduced by some percentage for being used goods. The formula is:

Value Range of Land + Range of Replacement Cost for Improvements (reduced by obsolescence and age) + Value range of amenities = the Range of Core Value Pricing.

Start with the land

Start by asking yourself what your land is worth without the house or any improvements. You want to determine a high/low range of land value. If yours is a two or four acre lot, what are similar lots selling for? If it is waterfront, what is the going rate per foot? If it is a large land tract, for how much have similar land tracts sold?

If, by chance, there is no past sale, say for seven acres of waterfront because none has been available for twenty years, that is important to note. Scarcity adds value (more about that later). In this instance, use the last similar land sales and adjust them for location and inflation. For instance, if you know the historical appreciation rates in that area, adjust the sales using those rates. (On the *GetYourHighestPrice.com* website you can subscribe to a Home Appreciator tool that will allow you to do this easily.) Your agent may find other sales where you may infer a land value, for instance, where homes were bought to be torn down. However you choose to do it, you must begin by determining a range of value for just the land. Remember, it can be aggressive, but it must be credible and defensible and expressed as a range because values are always inexact moving targets.

The issue with high rise condos and coops in cities

City properties would seem to defy this starting point. After all, how do you allocate the land value to a condo or a coop on Park Avenue and 90th Street in New York or on the ocean in Miami Beach? True, some idea of land value can be garnered from past sales or at least the assessment by municipal authorities, but allocating it among the units in a building can be difficult since a greater proportion of value can come from vertical factors. Nonetheless, determining a Core Value range can sometimes be easier with urban properties since the per square foot prices paid embody the underlying land value and the vertical adjustments for height and views. Thus, the calculation of land value can often be skipped altogether and you should focus instead on the replacement cost.

Add the replacement cost

Second, after either determining your land value or, if you live in a high rise building, skipping this step, you need to know what it costs to replace your home. To find out, ask your agent what are the building costs per square foot in your market. If your agent does not know, have the agent ask three separate builders who specialize in affordable, middle market, and luxury housing. They will know in an instant. Why, should you talk to builders servicing the affordable and middle market when you have a luxury home? Simple. It gives you a sense of how low building costs can be in your market. For instance, here in Greenwich, builders routinely will say it costs $300 to $500 per square foot to build a luxury home. But it usually comes as a shock to learn that affordable builders can build a home for $150-$175 a square foot. Elsewhere building costs can easily run under $100 per square foot. Knowing how affordably homes can be built in your market helps put into perspective what the luxury builders are telling you. We also recommend that you talk with two or three homeowners who have recently constructed a house because they will know the range of building costs. Your efforts should result in a consensus opinion as to the likely range. Once you know the upper, middle and lower range of replacement cost per square foot, multiply those dollar amounts by the approximate square footage you are offering. That is the range of likely replacement value for your home.

Once again, city properties (condos and coops) are a little easier because replacement value is the selling price of new construction in your market, a figure that is usually easily determined by visiting several new construction projects in your neighbourhood.

Add the amenity value

Third, you are going to add the value of your amenities which include luxuries like a pool, tennis court, guest house, landscaping, waterfalls, fencing, an outdoor spa, night lighting, entry gates, alarm systems, etc. For city properties these include the finishes, the views, access to parking, common areas, concierge and doorman services, etc. But the amenities can also include mundane, but necessary items like septic systems, wells, driveways, retaining walls, site preparation, etc. Among them can also be the "requisite qualities" that qualify it as luxury real estate (see our Appendix for a more detailed discussion). List your amenities and then put a ballpark price range on each of them.

After ascertaining a range of land value, a range of reasonable construction costs and a range of amenity values, you are ready to finish your first step in creating a Core Value Pricing range. Remember each of these components is not a fixed number, but a range and, therefore, the resulting adjusted Core Value will be a range, too.

Step 2. Adjust for specific factors associated with your property that add value and others that limit value

Once you arrive at an initial range of Core Value, fine tune the key factors that affect the value: land, improvements and amenities. The land can be adjusted up or down for:

Upward factors	Downward factors
Abuts conservation land	Near highway noise
Superior privacy	Near another home
Flat nice lot	Wetlands on or near property+
Hilly lot	Clearly inferior neighbors
No record of any area sales	

Similarly, the improvements and amenities can be adjusted up or down for:

Upward factors	Downward factors
Slate roof	Eight maid's rooms
Superior finishes	No air conditioning
Least expensive house in area	Most expensive house in area
Views	Design flaws
Beauty	Dated
Feng shui	Feng shui

Each market is different. A positive factor in one market can be a negative in another. You may have to adjust up or down for dozens of variables in your local market known only to you and your agent.

Adjust the replacement cost for age

After arriving at the replacement cost range for your home, one of the largest adjustments will be reducing it by some amount for age or what is called "obsolescence." It is, after all, used goods. Depending on the local demand in the market for new or old, we generally give a home a forty-year life. This may seem relatively short for most real estate markets, but we have found that luxury buyers discount homes heavily for age, more so than buyers in the general market. Maybe they do this because they are too busy to do much work on a home, or maybe it is just that they can afford anything and therefore prefer new. For whatever reason, after forty years, most luxury homes have lost a good deal of value. (Note: while the house, i.e. the improvements, may lose value, the underlying value of the lot usually rises due to increasing scarcity of buildable land). You can certainly use a higher figure than our forty year life, especially if you are selling a home that has been meticulously maintained over the years. Just consult with your agent and disclose the number you are using and be ready to defend it.

Let's create an example using a ten-year old home and the forty year figure for obsolescence. If we determine it costs $2M to replace the home, take the $2M replacement cost, divide by forty years and get a yearly deduction for age and obsolescence of $50,000 ($2M divided by forty years = $50,000 a year). Then, multiply this figure by the age of the home, in this case 10 years ($50,000 x ten years of age = a reduction from replacement cost of $500,000). This nets a value for the improvements adjusted for obsolescence of $1.5M ($2M less $500,000 for obsolescence).

Unfortunately, this does not work well for antique homes or for those that have been meticulously maintained. If a home is in perfect condition, it may have to be valued at the same price as new. It also does not work well for homes with spectacular detail that would cost a fortune to replace (a castle or a palace, for example). Such details should not be valued at their replacement cost. No one will pay it. Therefore, you lose credibility by suggesting someone should. I In addition, fine craftsmanship often incurs high maintenance costs that negatively affect value.

But for most luxury properties, the preceding formula works.

Adjust the amenity value, too

Now apply the same kind of up or down adjustment for age and obsolescence to your amenities (with the exception of landscaping which can actually increase in value over time as mature landscaping can have greater value than new). Don't fuss too much on pricing exactitude at this stage. Rather, the operative question always is: how much would someone value this amenity today in its present condition?

There are three other values that can have applicability to your property. The first is "convenience value."

The convenience value

This is extra value that comes from a property in turn-key condition. In resort and second-home markets like Lake Tahoe, Miami Beach, Vail or the Hamptons of Long Island, properties sometimes trade with a substantial convenience value. This is due to the seasonal nature of the market. For example, someone buying a Hamptons home in April does not want to wait six months to move in. They want to buy it, move in and throw a party over Memorial Day. In such markets, if applicable, adjust upward for convenience value. Be aware that this is a highly subjective adjustment and you should not get too carried away with it. Also, "move in" condition usually means something very different to you, the homeowner, than it does to a prospective buyer.

Celebrity value

Another reason why luxury buyers in some markets pay more is celebrity value. Usually this involves being able to say one owns "so and so's" home. Buyers often enjoy the associated bragging rights. This, too, is a highly subjective adjustment and it can work in reverse. If some notorious deed or death taints your property, its value can be negatively affected and you should adjust down, too.

Scarcity (or rarity) value

"Few of a kind" or "one of a kind" properties offer an adjustment for scarcity value. The scarcity of waterfront parcels or large landed tracts (especially where available sub-divisible land is rare), can add substantially to your Core Value. Given the lack of comparable data for such properties (it, too, is scarce), the subjectivity of this adjustment is great and therefore a large scale upward adjustment can be dangerous in terms of overpricing. Similarly, "one of a kind" properties can also mean "out of date" and may require a downward adjustment. After all, there may be a reason why such properties are "one of a kind" and no one builds them anymore.

At this point, you should have an Adjusted Core Value Pricing range. If you wish assistance in calculating your Core Value, ask your agent to use our Core Value Pricing Calculator available on our website: *http://GetYourHighestPrice.com* or you can go there and purchase its use for yourself.

Participate with your agent

We urge you to participate in this whole exercise with your agent. It should take only a few minutes. Remember in Step 1 you are not looking for precision. The price you get will not usually exceed replacement value. Why, after all, would anyone pay more than new for something that isn't new? It is in Step 2 that you begin the process of narrowing and adjusting.

An example of a Core Valuation band

To provide an example of the end product of Steps 1 and 2, let's imagine a property that is ten years old with a 7000 square foot home on two acres of land, swimming pool, 500 foot driveway and decent landscaping. We determine that a two-acre lot in the area is worth between $700,000 and $900,000 and a new luxury home can be built for $250 to $350 per square foot. Pools run about $75,000 to $100,000 and the driveway runs about $70 to $90 per foot ($35,000 to $45,000 for a 500 foot driveway).

Adding this up results in an initial Core Value range as follows:

Range of Land Value:	$700,000	to	$900,000	
Replacement Value of Improvements:				
House:	$1,750,000	to	$2,450,000	+
Pool:	$75,000	to	$100,000	+
Driveway:	$35,000	to	$45,000	=
Total Replacement Value of Improvements:	$1,860,000	to	$2,595,000	
Reduction in Improvements for age:	(465,000)	to	(648,750)	
Resulting Range-Core Value Improvements:	$1,395,000	to	$1,946,250	
Range of Core Value with Land	$2,095,000	to	$2,846,250	

Not including the land, we have a replacement value for the improvements of between $1,860,000 and $2,595,000. Using our 40 year life for improvements, reduce that value by 2.5% a year or 25% for the 10 years of age. This reduces the value of the improvements by $465,000 to $648,750. The resulting range of $2,095,000 on the low end ($1,860,000 reduced by $465,000 + Land of $700,000 = $2,095,000) to $2,846,250 on the high end ($2,595,000 reduced by $648,750 + Land of $900,000 = $2,846,250) is the estimated Core Value replacement range for this property. Note how wide this range can be.

> Discounts to core value are what savvy, value conscious buyers always want. So give it to them.

Discount the Core Value Pricing

In the first two steps we are only dealing with the replacement cost, with some modest reduction for the property being used goods. Some agents fear that such a calculation will result in a high figure that, in turn, will inflate your expectations of value. They may also feel that it is all irrelevant because it has nothing to do with the reality of what is going on in the market.

We assure you that we know this objection and agree with the potential criticism. But what we are doing here is something else. We are using a technique used extensively in merchandising many products. We are establishing a high, but credible, initial replacement value and then demonstrating that your property offers a discount to that value. By doing so we raise comfort by demonstrating value and we help to create a rationale for purchase. We also get the marketing sound-bite or elevator speech that helps us to attract initial interest. It is, after all, discounts to Core Value that smart, savvy and sophisticated buyers always want. So give it to them. We will return to this idea again in Step 6.

Step 3. Look to past sales in the luxury market

In Steps 3-4 the reality that exists in the marketplace will begin to sink in and affect your pricing thoughts. While you need the discount sound-bite we mentioned above, you also need to have your expectations tempered by the reality of what buyers are willing to pay. In this third step you will get from your agent a list of every sale defined as luxury in your area. The list should include at least two years worth of sales. If prices in your area are in decline, cover at least a year before the peak of the market (the list could extend back five years or more). Rank the sales from highest to lowest. This can be done in Excel.

Ranking from most to least expensive instantly shows you the whole market. Take your Adjusted Core Value range and insert it into this ranking. This list of ranked properties will instantly put your value into perspective. You now can ask: Is it as good as the sale ranked above it? Is it better than the sale ranked below it? Does it compare favorably with the sales around it? If not, why not? By ranking your Core Value you can visually see exactly where your property fits into the past sales market.

While this process sounds pretty simple, in reality it can be difficult. Take for example a horse farm in Virginia or a waterfront home on Cape Cod. A broker must research the values of farms throughout Virginia or the price per front foot of waterfront all around Cape Cod. These types of properties require a database and expertise far outside a narrow local market. If you find an agent with such expertise, think seriously about interviewing them. Such agents have the data you need.

Step 4. What else is available?

Fourth, look to see what else is currently available, i.e. the competition. Your agent can easily pull all the data from the MLS and rank the offerings from highest asking price to lowest. Think about where your property might fall within these rankings. The buyer will view your property within this context, and therefore, you should, too. And, frankly, you should do it before the buyer does by having your agent take you to view these competitive properties. After all, these are the properties the buyer is going to see. Also, you should continue to assess your competition monthly by asking your agent to take you to see new competitive listings. Doing so is a good reality check for you and allows you to always know what the buyers will see.

Step 5. Look to third parties

There are several indicators of value from third parties that you must reference during your pricing deliberations. These are entities that have already tried to determine the value of your property. Because they are independent, the buyers will find credibility in their estimates.

Assessed Value

This is what the local taxing authority thinks the property is worth. Assessed value can be 100% of fair market valuation, 70%, 50% or whatever. Because local taxing authorities do not want to waste valuable time in taxpayer appeals, they often spend a great deal of time trying to determine accurately what your property is worth. They can be very sensitive to values and don't want to value yours too high nor too low. A low valuation would only deprive the municipality of tax revenues tied to fair market value. A high value will only result in time-consuming appeals. Therefore, they carefully watch selling prices to provide a rational, defensible value at which to tax you. Learn from what they have researched.

The buyer-agent's CMA

Today, most buyers sign a contract to be represented by a buyer-agent. That agent in turn owes their fiduciary obligation, not to you, but to the buyer who hired them. One of the buyer-agent's responsibilities is to research the value of properties on which the buyer-client is bidding. That means the agent will do a traditional Comparable Market Analysis ("CMA") for their client. Needless to say, it takes some effort for a buyer to bid higher than what their buyer-agent's research indicates is fair value. Therefore, if a buyer-agent's CMA does not support the value you are asking, have your listing agent request a copy. The two of you can learn what the buyer-agents are telling their clients. Adjust accordingly.

The reasonable business person rule

The reasonable business person rule asks what every buyer will ask themselves: Will any reasonable business person pay what you expect? Would you? You didn't get to the point of owning such a fine property without being a smart, sharp business person. You will understand, therefore, that the market is made up of buyers like you. They are smart and value conscious.

Also, as we have already indicated, rich buyers hire advisors to make sure they don't make mistakes. Even if an impulse buyer were to fall in love with your property, he would go back to his lawyer or accountant, financial adviser or trust officer. Then the voice of reason enters the picture. Each will start asking key questions beginning with a defense of value. They will also order an appraisal in order to establish the price a reasonable business person would pay.

We can assure you that the buyer's advisors will do this if for no other reason than to keep control of the funds (financial managers usually get a 1-2 percent management fee). Releasing these funds reduces their pay.

As a seller, you cannot avoid the reasonable business person rule. So be prepared to defend the reasonableness of your value.

Appraised Value

We strongly urge you to have an appraisal done before the property is put on the market. During all "go go" periods in real estate, getting an appraisal falls out of favor. After all, why appraise something that is only going up in value? When the economy slows, however, it is critical to know in advance what the buyer will find out later. Additionally, if *you* order the appraisal *you* influence the outcome.

If you already have an appraisal done for insurance purposes or a net worth statement, consult it and provide it to your agent. Your agent can readily use the information to help build a credible and defensible value for your property.

The bank appraisal

The buyer may want to add leverage to the deal and take advantage of the deductibility of some mortgage interest. If the buyer finances a portion of the purchase, you are right back to getting an appraisal, only now it is for the bank or finance company. Thus, know that it is unlikely that you can escape getting an appraisal. It is only a question of when it gets done and who influences it, the buyer or you. Hire an appraiser in advance yourself so you can be the prime influence on the end product.

> In this way, other people's opinion of your value manifests itself many times: once by the tax assessors, once by the CMA done by the buyer-agent (and the appraisal they are sure to recommend), once by the reasonable business person rule and a final time by the appraisal for the financial institution. It is important, therefore, for you to consult each of these third party sources and know in advance what they are saying about your value.

Step 6: Raise comfort through discount pricing

After having established a Core Value in Steps 1 and 2, you will often arrive at a value that is far higher than the tempered expectations that Steps 3, 4 and 5 provide. If, therefore, we know that a Core Value pricing calculation may lead to an inflated value, why do we begin in this way? The reason is exactly as charged: it may lead to an inflated, but still credible and defensible value which you can in turn discount.

And by discounting it, you can provide the savvy buyer with a sense of getting the bargain he or she expects.

Thus, while most agents start valuing your property with past sales or current listing prices of available properties, we suggest you begin differently. As we demonstrated earlier, we recommend breaking down the value of the improvements into what it would fairly cost to replace and then reduce that amount for obsolescence, fully realizing that doing so can often provide a much higher figure than past sales and comparable properties suggest. Then we want to offer buyers a discount to that higher figure. Demonstrating a generous Core Value to a buyer and showing them how much of a discount from Core Value you are asking, cultivates a reason for buyers to act. This is not a step that occurs in the auction, except at the opening when many hands rise in the hope of getting a discounted bargain below the value range. It is rather a marketing technique common to all merchandizing. Buyers act on emotion and then rationalize with logic. We want to give them the logic to rationalize their purchase by giving them a discount. By discounting that elevated Core Value figure and by enveloping it within the comfort of getting a bargain, luxury buyers are more at ease to act.

Are they going to believe the calculation? Probably not. Nonetheless, it will still make them feel better that such value has been pointed out. By walking them through what it would cost to replace everything in your property and adjusting that price for age and then discounting further by some percentage, you have helped to provide comprehensive, yet credible and defensible value and a reason for buyers to act. Recall that this is why you (and your agent) should not be concerned if the Core Value is an elevated number. You are going to discount from it.

Getting offers and avoiding Sole Buyer Syndrome

By creating and providing a discount, you have also done something else. You have raised buyers' comfort during that critical early period of marketing, that time in the first few weeks before there are any offers. This is the time when you need to establish that someone wants this property. At this early stage you have primarily value to sell and you need this discount to entice buyers to bid and thereby supply you with the crucial early offers needed to establish that someone wants your property. In this way, you also avoid Sole Buyer Syndrome.

To summarize: start with generously calculated (and adjusted) Core Value Pricing which you then discount initially to provide your savvy, value-conscious buyers with what they are seeking, a bargain. As you will see in Chapter 13 on the sale of Clarendon Court in Newport, Rhode Island, articulating a discount to Core Value can provide interesting and unexpected results. Why? Because when you talk 'discount' and 'bargain,' you are now speaking a language the rich understand. That is why you begin with Core Value Pricing.

Step 7: Setting the asking price

Now that you've determined the Core Value Pricing range, adjusted it for all the variables, correlated it to past sales, compared it to currently available properties, created (with your agent) the high and low range of likely valuation and articulated a credible, defensible value that has been discounted from replacement cost (but is still in line with past sales, currently available properties and third party opinions), it's time to settle on the asking price.

If you are in an up market with prices rising steadily, you can be more aggressive and price at the higher end of the valuation range. If you are in a down market, focus more on the Core Value versus past sales and then discount from it to interest buyers. Above all, make sure you have a defensible value for the smart, sophisticated buyer to whom you are appealing. Steps 1-6 of this process should now make Step 7 easy. In the end, pricing must be high enough that you do not feel you are leaving money on the table, but it must be credible and defensible enough to attract agents and buyers to your property.

Finally, the asking price of a property is like a lure on a fishing line: if it doesn't attract any fish, change the lure. The asking price is only as good as the buyers it attracts.

Give your listing agent enough time to do proper pricing

While you should certainly tell agents your thoughts on pricing (they will want to hear them), pricing is too important an issue to decide without thorough research, discussion and time, as this chapter should demonstrate. Therefore, don't be impatient if your listing agent doesn't want to talk pricing on the first visit and instead wants to get back to you. In fact, be suspicious if an agent talks pricing on their first visit because it can mean they have not spent much time considering it. In addition, please be advised that we have often signed an agreement to list a home with a client who liked our marketing and sales expertise, but with whom we have not yet agreed on price. That section of the listing agreement was just left blank or we wrote in "to be determined by mutual agreement." If we could not agree on price, the agreement was null and void.

Pricing can take up to a week. An agent should do the research, work with you to determine your Core Value Pricing, visit some past sales or properties currently on the market, come up with a range within which a sale will likely occur and put all that together into a Comparable Market Analysis (CMA). The agent may also want to call upon the opinions of other agents and ask you for permission to bring them for a preview. Their opinions can often provide an early indication of how the market will react to your property.

Again, be patient with this pricing process. Get in your agent's car and visit what buyers will be viewing before and after they see your house. You must know your competition. Doing this helps to give you the buyer's perspective. It also allows you and the agent to look at the same data set.

In the end, the asking price should be within a credible and defensible valuation band and demonstrate a discount to Core Value in line with past sales, current competitive properties for sale and third party opinions. Your agent should be able to convey the asking price with conviction to a buyer within 30 seconds.

The Takeaway

Luxury pricing is highly elastic, difficult to assess, and never fixed. The "Seven Step" process to arrive at an asking price is:

1. **Establish a range of Core Value** for the property based upon the formula:

    Range of Land Value + Replacement Cost for Improvements + Amenities - Obsolescence and Age = a range of Core Value Pricing.

2. **Adjust the Core Value Pricing range for factors specific to your property** that add value and others that limit value. Also, adjust for any "convenience value," "celebrity value," or "scarcity value."

3. **Compare this range to past sales** to see where it places the property and make any additional adjustments based upon those sales.

4. **Compare the range to the competition** currently on the market to determine where your pricing should be positioned *vis a vis* those other options for buyers.

5. **See what third parties say about value** such as the tax assessors and an appraiser. Remind yourself that buyers are just as smart as sellers and tend to follow a reasonable business person rule. Get an appraisal before the buyer does.

6. **Establish a discount to Core Value** to entice buyers to bid by raising their comfort level with a perceived bargain. This discount to Core Value will be your agent's elevator speech and your 30 second commercial for the property (read the stories in Chapters 12 and 13).

7. **Set the asking price with your agent** fully informed of the risks and rewards of the high and low range of Core Value Pricing. The asking price is only as good as the number of buyers it attracts.

Chapter 5: Allow Marketing to Get You the Highest Price

The final step in pricing has nothing to do with articulating or defending value. Rather, it has 100% to do with marketing. In Chapter 3 we mentioned the need for your agent to create a competitive market for your property by orchestrating two or more buyers to bid simultaneously or create the threat thereof. We mentioned that such a threat can come from an agent's reputation for marketing success, from competitive pricing and from buyers knowing of other buyers' interest. We emphasized that a power marketer understands their job is to raise buyer (and agent) comfort to bid while keeping the fear of loss ever-present. Always, we argued your marketer needed to prevent the onset of Sole Buyer Syndrome. In this chapter, we want to focus on how such marketing affects value and gets you the highest price. First, some "do not's" before the must "do's."

Bringing one buyer (and the accompanying danger of doing so)

When you first list your property, do not allow an agent to cut a deal to bring in that one buyer known only to that agent who they claim is just itching to buy your property. Some agents even cut their commission to lure you into taking this bait.

Interest does not sell property. Competition or the threat of competition does. Here is what happens to that buyer who the agent is claiming wants to buy your property (and often is "sure" they will): once they realize that they got a special first look and are without competition, it is likely they will say 'no, thank you' and move on.

Allowing one agent to bring their one buyer in an un-orchestrated single shot showing is a bad idea. One buyer does not create the competitive market needed to get the highest price. Remember that everyone wants something more when they know others want it. At a minimum you have now wasted valuable ammunition because this is a buyer who could have been seen by other buyers at initial showings and might have raised other buyer's comfort, possibly to act. Instead of getting the maximum number of buyers looking at your property at the same time, you have allowed your property to dribble onto the market and you have diluted the fear of loss and the possibility of competition, the opposite of what you want. Worse, by allowing one buyer into the property, word always gets out. It is not the agent who tells other agents, but the buyer. Finally, someone getting an insider's first look only serves to offend agents, the very people in the market who you do not want to offend because it is they as a group who have 95%-100% of the buyers.

Once you fall for the "I have this one perfect buyer" line you will have started your marketing process by default rather than by design.

Getting Record Prices

If you have a property that could get a record price, consider a few points. First, know that every agent wants to get a record price. Getting record prices is the icing on the real estate agent's cake. Big sales and high prices are part of the ethos of the luxury real estate world. But getting a record price is only possible under the right conditions.

David's down market blues

Getting a record price in a down market is very difficult, if not impossible. I once tried to do this in October 1987 by bringing to market one of the most expensive properties in the United States, "Harbour Point" on Center Island in Oyster Bay, New York. Priced at $26M, the property consisted of a main house plus eight other buildings on a twenty-five acre waterfront peninsula within a gated community abutting some thirty acres of conservation land. It is hard to imagine a property with more of the makings of a record sale.

The day before the Tuesday open house the stock market crashed, falling 22 percent in a single day. On that grim Tuesday morning, all I could do was pretend that the world had not changed. But it had. I was now trying to market something for which the possibility of success was slim to none. Even worse, my sellers were extremely upbeat and confident in my ability to market their property.

In the end, I did produce an $18M cash offer which the sellers did not accept, as their expectations were too high. The market did not fully recover for six years, during which time the listing expired and they chose not to re-list. Years later the property ended up transferring far below the original asking price. So much for a valiant effort to score a record sale during a down market, even with the best of properties.

While there are occasions in down markets when getting a record sale is possible, this usually involves properties with huge celebrity or rarity value. Even then, down markets create an atmosphere of bargain hunting. Seeking a record price in a down market is usually not worth your time and effort.

The pleasures of up markets

During up markets, getting a record price is at least possible if you have the right mix of qualities such as waterfront land abutting conservation land, a pedigree or history, views, location in a premier luxury community, celebrity or rarity value.

Second, the property requires an agent who knows *power marketing* techniques such as filling the room with as many agents and would-be buyers as possible, coordinated sequential showings, and extensive broker marketing (including open houses).

Third, the agent must know how to create competition and raise the comfort level of the buyers by orchestrating them to a point in time of having two or more bidding simultaneously.

If you don't have any of these, an up market can still produce a record sale, but it is likely to be due to a rising tide lifting all ships with a dose of old fashioned good luck.

Who might bid the highest: the case of abutters

Sometimes the highest bidder for a property is literally right next door. Allow your agent to contact your neighbors, especially abutters, about your property. Abutters, like most neighbours, always want to know what is going on next door. Sometimes they are the buyer who has the willingness to pay the most for your property. For example, they may want your property to sell for a good price to provide a high comparable sale for their own. Paying up for your property helps secure a kind of financial protection for their value. Or, buying your property provides a buffer of physical protection for theirs. Or, they may just want to control who their neighbor might be.

But the most compelling reason for abutters to pay up for your property is that when it is combined with theirs, the result can often be greater value than each property separately. For instance, when someone has ¾ of an acre of land in a half-acre zone and can buy the property next door which also has ¾ of an acre, they may be able to get three half-acre lots out of the two parcels and thereby create extra land value. The same is true with vertical living in condo towers, as in Chicago, New York or Miami Beach. If an adjacent apartment or one above or below comes to market, the value to neighbors in owning additional bedrooms or space can be greater. Because of these many reasons abutters are often the most emotional and impulsive of buyers with the greatest financial incentive to pay you a record price. Make sure they are contacted by your agent as part of an orchestrated marketing campaign.

First offers can be your best offers

A second group who can help you to get the highest price are those first offerors. As discussed in Chapter 3, the old real estate agents' adage is true: your first offer is often your best.

First offers usually come from buyers who have been in the market for awhile and already know that nothing else fits their desire. Because of this they are prepared to act more quickly. They also may be weary of the search process and be afraid of losing another property. Because they do not know how many other buyers are interested in yours, that uncertainty poses the greatest threat. Therefore, how first offerors are handled is important to getting a good price and even a record price. Many a seller has become emboldened when they get a good price right away and dismiss it, fearing that the property is under-priced. By the third or fourth week on the market, the initial threat dissipates and the buyers stop thinking about aggressive bidding. If you stall a good first offer you may realize, too late, that there are no other buyers. If there are no other buyers, the initial threat is gone and the first buyer may be gone, too, or at least is likely to pull back.

Making buyer interest known

Unlike the auction, the real estate marketing process is a more veiled endeavor. But as we have indicated, if there is to be any hope of instilling a fear of loss into the process or raising buyers' comfort to avoid Sole Buyer Syndrome, buyers need to know of other interest. To convey such interest your agent can take the following actions (see also Chapter 12, the story of *Le Domaine Resistance*).

First, your agent can create a threat by sharing the marketing plan for the property (orally is fine) with other brokers, including how many open houses are planned, the number of mailings and ads that are being placed, the variety of websites where it can be found, how many agents have been included in the sale, public relations or special events, etc.

Second, your agent must convey the belief that the property will be sold, that there will be a deal here for some buyer to buy and for an agent to earn a commission. This, of course, requires you to be serious about selling. Agents and buyers prefer to deal with someone who wants to sell rather than someone who is just 'testing the market.' Confidence that the property will sell also suggests that the listing agent may have a good sense of the buyer demand for the property. The threat of such demand can move others to act.

Third, showings should be grouped sequentially to the maximum extent possible. For instance, three showings could be booked at 10 a.m., 11 a.m. and Noon. In this way, the 10 a.m. buyer sees the 11 a.m. buyer arrive and the 11 a.m. buyer sees the 10 a.m. leaving and the Noon buyer arrive. Such sequential showings help to convey that there is real interest in the property.

Fourth, e-blasts that keep every agent up-to-date about showings or the number of offers are ideal, easy and cheap. Similarly, putting this information into the MLS listing notes can be helpful since agents tend to read those notes diligently.

Why you want low offers

Just as the auctioneer begins the auction process by encouraging low bids at the start, so too, to get the highest price you must not only tolerate low initial bids, but encourage and welcome them. In Chapter 12 you will see an example of the power of low bids. But here let's just review why the auctioneer welcomes them and you should, too.

Your agent's initial goal is to fill the room so as to demonstrate that many buyers want your property. Next, that desire must be formulated into specific offers, just as at the onset of an auction the auctioneer encourages low offers. This is done to concretely demonstrate desire for the object being auctioned. You must mimic this practice. Of course, you do not have to accept any of the offers, but, ideally, within the first four weeks of marketing, you want to get 1-3 offers regardless of how low they are. Why is this so important?

To understand the answer, try to recall the last time you saw a property that you were interested in buying and try to remember the conversation that ensued. We bet your conversation was not dissimilar from that of most buyers when they are interested. It goes something like this:

> Buyer: "So what's the price on this property again?"
> Agent: "$3,560,000."
> Buyer: "And how long has it been on the market?"
> Agent: "Four weeks."
> Buyer: "Have there been any offers?"

When asked, "Have there been any offers?" you always want your agent to be able honestly to say: "Yes, there have been several, but none of them has been high enough to take the property. Maybe yours will be."

Consider, for instance, the alternative answer: "No, there have been no offers."

Which one do you think gets a buyer willing to bid and willing to bid more?

In this way, offers, even low offers, help create a positive psychology to the sale and raise the comfort of buyers to act by validating the wisdom of their interest in the property. No matter how smart or how rich or how sophisticated buyers are, they need such validation. It is therefore imperative that they get it and the best way to obtain it is to encourage all offers, even very low offers to establish that someone wants your property, just like the auctioneer does at a luxury auction.

Finally, nothing conveys interest more than making the Last Call. Therefore, let's turn to this all important marketing action.

The Last Call

Making the Last Call is the most effective means of getting the best price in any market at any time and in any price range. In luxury marketing, it is the one essential *power marketing* action step with the greatest chance of achieving the highest price. When you have offers on a property and you feel a deal may be near, your agent should call all the other agents who have expressed any interest in or shown the property and inform them that there is now "serious buyer interest." Then they should ask those agents if their buyers are still interested. If so, your agent should tell them to come forward now or they are likely to lose the property. In particular abutters and first offerors should be re-contacted.

Your agent is, in effect, the auctioneer. By making this Last Call, your agent is creating a competitive process and respecting most buyers' desire to have a last shot. Recall the story about our own resort property where we netted 19% more when our listing agent noted an accepted offer in the MLS. As a result an initial buyer became aware that we had an offer, albeit accidentally. In this situation the agent effectively made the Last Call by default rather than by design. While we certainly would have preferred it was done by design, at least it ended in a sale at a price 19% higher than the previous offer.

As a result of the Last Call you will (1) get a good idea if there is any more market interest, (2) will know if you can get to that all-important goal of multiple buyers bidding simultaneously, (3) probably get some second or third showings, if only because buyers come back "just to make sure the property is not for us," (4) create buzz around your property by indicating there is action. You will also (5) help most buyer-agents who will appreciate the call because now they have a reason to call their buyers again about your property. This courtesy call further helps buyer-agents to convey to their clients that markets are moving. As mentioned before, it is buyers not receiving this call that often infuriates them enough to complain to the manager's office.

> Making the Last Call is the most effective means of getting the best price, in any market at any time and in any price range. In luxury marketing, it is the one essential power marketing action step that will achieve the highest price.

By recommending the Last Call, we are not advocating shopping anyone's offer. That would be breaching what in today's real estate process is considered confidential information and it would only anger both agent and their buyer. All we advocate is what the auctioneer does: tell everyone that serious interest has been expressed and the marketing and sales process is coming to an end.

> Making the Last Call results in activity or a buzz around a property.

Give everyone a last chance to participate, if they wish. Needless to say, no agent should ever make this call without *truly* having "serious interest."

If we had our druthers, instituting the Last Call would be a new article in the Code of Ethics of the National Association of Realtors.® Very few actions generate more value for a seller than making the Last Call and nothing better confirms to all parties the fairness of the process. Let's close with a second illustration of the Last Call, this time how Linda netted 25% more for her sellers, not by default but by *power marketing* design.

Linda's *power marketing* story

Linda had a $1.27M listing in Greenwich which had little to no activity. The sellers were not only close friends, but had already transferred to California. They were sitting with a vacant house anxious to sell.

After months of showings, Linda finally got a $975,000 offer on the property. She called the sellers, who were so willing to sell that they were prepared to take the offer. But she told them to wait until she performed the ritual of the Last Call.

She then called all eighteen agents who had shown the property and told them about the serious interest she had. Within two days there were five additional showings, three buyers who had seen it before and two new buyers, all generated by the buzz of activity from her call. The result was a new bid for $1.025M. She then received a succession of bids, which after several weeks of negotiations, resulted in the seller getting $1.210M for the property. The Last Call resulted in her client receiving more than two hundred thousand dollars above the first bid for the property (almost 25% more).

This is the value added by making the Last Call. This is how we agents can both get the highest price and maintain the highest ethic while fulfilling our fiduciary responsibilities to you. Finally, this is how agents should present the competition to buyers, liberate them from the fear of bidding, unleash their desire to win and, because of the transparency and inherent fairness of the process, also keep them happy.

Making the Last Call vividly illustrates again how the price you get is a function of the marketing you choose. Making the Last Call demonstrates all the principles of the auction's competition. You will see the effectiveness of the Last Call again in the two stories that make up Chapters 12 and 13 on *Le Domaine Resistance* and Clarendon Court.

These Do's and Don'ts are important demonstrations of how proper marketing and competition or the threat thereof, can and does contribute heavily to your getting the highest price.

The Takeaway

- Avoid the trap of asking your agent to bring just one buyer before the marketing begins.

- Getting a record price is almost impossible in a down market.

- Getting a record price is largely reserved for up markets and for properties that have the right mix of qualities.

- Abutters are important potential buyers who may buy the property for themselves or know someone who they have always wanted as a neighbour. They should be contacted when the marketing commences and as part of the ritual of the Last Call.

- An abutter often has the strongest incentive to pay the highest price because combining their property with yours can mean 1 + 1 = 3.

- As soon as a marketing campaign begins, potential buyers experience the greatest uncertainty about its likely success and thus provide you a narrow window during which fear of loss is present. Because of it, a first offer can be your best offer.

- Encourage all offers, even low offers, because you must avoid Sole Buyer Syndrome by demonstrating that someone (hopefully many) want the property at some price.

- Make buyer interest as public as possible without violating each buyer's privacy.

- Making the Last Call is the most effective means of stimulating buyer interest and offers the best hope of getting the highest price.

Chapter 6: How to Hire an Agent

Now you know that to sell for the highest price, you have to orchestrate as many buyers as possible into a competitive situation. To find those buyers and implement that orchestration, you need the right agent.

How most owners choose an agent

If you are like most consumers, you tend to hire an agent that you like. You probably do this because you think that all agents are the same anyways. Therefore, you might as well hire someone likeable and, hopefully, trustworthy. Or, you might hire an agent because you want someone with greater than local reach. Thus, you might be attracted to some of the national and international franchises because you want to access the people

> Don't list with a friend if they cannot demonstrate the expertise you need to get the highest price.

73

in their network. You then assess the individual agent's professionalism and how they carry themselves. You may also hire someone based upon their track record or that of their firm, looking at market share and whether they specialize in what you are trying to sell.

The MLS: the best network

Interestingly, the argument that you should choose an agent with a network is probably one of the least useful criteria. Why? Because all agents have networks of some kind, either personal and local or as part of their belonging to luxury marketing groups, national and international referral groups, franchise networks or independent agent networks. In effect, everyone is in a network and your trying to evaluate which one is going to have your buyer will be an exercise in futility. What you want to do is access all the networks to which the agents in your market belong, not just one. As we will show you in the next chapter, when you list your property with a broker who is a member of the Multiple Listing Service ("MLS"), you get the benefit of *everyone's* network, not just that of your listing agent. Thus, every agent who puts a listing into the MLS gets the benefit of everyone else's network, as do you.

What to look for

To determine who to hire, first remind yourself that you are hiring a salesperson. If you are thinking of hiring a friend or a member of the club, ask yourself if they know anything about marketing and sales. While they may be a good tennis partner or travel companion, that is not what you are hiring. You want someone who knows how to sell. As a successful businessperson, you may have a sales background yourself. If so, you know that a super salesperson requires an understanding of psychology few possess. While a real estate agent who is also a friend is someone you are likely to trust and your trust in them will form the bedrock of your brokerage relationship, ideally, you will hire someone you trust AND someone who understands how to get you the highest price. If they are not always one in the same, they can be.

Second, the salesperson you choose must understand the thinking we are describing here. If they don't, then give them this book or its companion written just for agents, **Power Marketing for Luxury Real Estate** available at *http://PowerMarketing.pro.* What is in both books is not hard to grasp and you will be doing your friend's career much good. They need *power marketing* techniques for their success and yours. You also might want to do this before you list with them.

Hopefully, your agent/friend gave you this book. In that case, you are both now on the same page. Don't list with a friend if they cannot demonstrate the expertise you need to get the highest price. Wait for them to correct their thinking. They can quickly read this or the above book or listen to our webinars and tele-seminars. They will be better agents for it.

The all-important, vital, powerful, indispensable other agents

The third requirement in hiring an agent is to find one with an inclusive mindset. Because 95% to 100% of the buyers for your property are going to come through other agents in the MLS, the one you hire must have an inclusive mindset and get along well with other members of the MLS. The agent must be willing to exclude no one from the sale, even including those beyond your local market. Indeed, your listing agent's primary job is to expose your property to as many agents as possible. This is done not just through the local MLS, but also regional or state-wide MLS services, national websites and by actively offering the property to luxury agents in key complementary markets and making sure they are invited into the sale. Because of the interconnectedness of wealthy buyers and their transcontinental neighborliness, a buyer for your property may be sitting in the hands of a distant agent.

This inclusive mindset also applies to you. If you don't like something about an agent out in the community, get over it. Right now you are trying to sell a house and you don't want to make enemies or reignite old wars. Rather, you and your listing agent are out to make friends in the brokerage community, lots of them. Because of the small size of the luxury market, every listing needs all the help and exposure possible from everyone in it.

David's CASE STUDY: Of shabby chic real estate agents

Years ago, I listed Sunninghill Farm in Brookville, Long Island, New York for $6.5M. It was home to the co-owners of Seattle Slew, the Triple Crown racehorse, and other champions, set on twenty-eight gorgeous acres in a two-acre zone within easy access to expressways into New York City.

One Sunday afternoon, I received a call from an agent whose name I did not recognize. She told me that there was a man in a long stretch limousine outside her office who had seen our brochure for the property and wanted a showing that afternoon.

I learned that he was a Wall Street investment manager. I told the buyer that I hoped he understood that a showing could not be arranged without a banking and legal reference and verification of employment.

The buyer, in turn, agreed and said it was no problem.

He gave me his banker and lawyer's number and indicated that if I called, there would be someone there to verify who he was.

"But this is a Sunday." I said. "How can I call your banker today?"

He then indicated that the number he provided was his banker's home number. In addition, he offered to call the banker and alert him that I would be calling.

The banker was the president of the bank. The president asked me the price of the property after which he confirmed that this gentleman could well afford to pay it. I also called the buyer's attorney and he, too, confirmed that the buyer was who he said he was and would have no problem buying this property and paying all cash. Similarly, I called the buyer's office to confirm his employment. He was the CEO.

Fortunately, the owners were away and when I spoke with the caretaker of the estate, he said the house was in its usual immaculate condition and there would be no problem showing it on such short notice. Next, I called the showing agent, who lived locally, to see if she could be there. She could.

The property was shown. After several weeks of negotiations involving several other buyers, this gentleman ended up winning the property.

A while later I called the selling agent to congratulate her on producing the winning buyer. I asked if I could thank her in person. She agreed and asked to meet at the same office where the buyer had come that fateful Sunday.

What I found was a weed-filled lot at the corner of a state highway just off the Interstate. On it was an "office" the size of a backyard tool shed. In it was one desk with two chairs.

Obviously the buyer had turned off the highway and headed to the estate district, stopping in at the first real estate brokerage office he saw. But something else caught my eye. In the window was the color brochure we had produced for Sunninghill Farm that had been sent to all the agents. The broker/owner/sole agent had put the brochure in the window both to attract attention and no doubt even to suggest that it was her listing. At a minimum she wanted her firm to be associated with listings of this caliber.

It did not matter to us. My firm was always delighted for anyone to use its brochures for window dressing. All the firm cared about was finding as many buyers as possible.

That office remains in my memory to this day because it exemplifies how you never know from where a buyer will come. Here was a one-person office that no one would ever have thought could produce a $6M plus buyer, but it did.

Marketing asset: how other agents view your agent

Because the buyer for your property is likely to be sitting within the brokerage community, the fourth asset you are looking for in your agent is an excellent relationship with the rest of the brokerage community. Why? Because your agent's good relationship with other agents is a pre-requisite for your finding multiple buyers. If the buyers are in the hands of agents who don't want to work with yours, then you lose those buyers.

> Here was a one-person office that no one would ever have thought could produce a $6M plus buyer, but it did.

More sales have been lost than the real estate profession is willing to admit because an agent with a buyer didn't trust or want to work with a certain listing agent. Everyone in the industry knows an "agent from hell" with whom they cringe at the thought of working. Often, they are the agent who doesn't return phone calls, makes showings difficult, isn't straightforward with facts, and simply tries to keep other agents out of the deal. You as a homeowner must know that the good standing and respect of your agent is vitally important to your getting the highest price.

Recently a Greenwich agent told us a story about taking a buyer to a property listed by another agent. The listing agent was late. She did not have a plot plan or tax map of the property. She did not have the disclosure forms for the buyer, nor did she know when she would get them from the seller. When asked to view the second floor, the buyer's agent was told that there was no Certificate of Occupancy for that floor and the seller would not try to get one until he had a deal. As a consequence, he didn't want anyone viewing it.

The buyer-agent was embarrassed to have taken a highly qualified multi-million dollar buyer to a listing agent with no answers and little desire to provide them. Result: the buyer-agent vowed never to take another buyer to that listing agent again.

We urge you to focus on agents who are viewed positively by their peers. Agents can demonstrate their good relations with the brokerage community by getting testimonials from other agents. Those testimonials should be included in their personal marketing brochures and on their website. Yes, testimonials from former clients are valuable, but think of how powerful testimonials from competing agents can be!

Trainings, certifications and designations

One problem with the real estate brokerage industry is that there is a low bar for entry. Someone can take a licensing class in a couple of weeks (almost none of the content of which has anything to do with sales and marketing skills) and become a real estate salesperson and start selling. While such classes provide compliance with state laws and entitle one to practice, they do not even provide baseline skills on how to sell. Even after joining a firm and a local Board of Realtors and Multiple Listing Service, agents rarely acquire the skills needed to sell. These organizations will provide them orientation, a review of the Code of Ethics, teach them how to put listings on a website, into the MLS, etc. Again, there is nothing here about how to sell.

> Agents can demonstrate their good relations with the brokerage community by getting testimonials from other agents.

A firm who hires such an agent may have an elementary or even advanced sales training program, but all such training is usually voluntary. To require attendance can even violate the agent's independent contractor agreement. Thus, it is appropriate to ask an agent what professional sales training they have received.

Know also that there are many great real estate sales trainers, but because real estate brokerage is essentially a business that emphasizes controlling listings and relies on the MLS to get them sold, such professional trainers focus largely on how to list property as opposed to how to sell one. (As a matter of full disclosure, David, too, does training for getting listings and has authored a book, workbook and tapes titled "*Winning Listing Presentations, for life*.")

Therefore, begin your inquiry into an agent's post-licensing professional development by asking if they have any designations, often offered by the National Association of Realtors® ("NAR") or the State and local Boards of Realtors. For residential agents, they include:

- Accredited Buyer's Representative (ABR)
- Accredited Land Consultant (ALC)
- Certified International Property Specialist (CIPS)
- Certified Property Manager (CPM)
- Certified Real Estate Brokerage Manager (CRB)
- Certified Residential Specialist (CRS)
- General Accredited Appraiser (GAA)
- NAR's Green Designation
- Graduate, Realtor Institute (GRI)
- Performance Management Network (PMN)
- Residential Accredited Appraiser (RAA)
- Seniors Real Estate Specialist (SRES)
- At Home With Diversity certification, (AHWD)
- Brokers Price Opinion Resource, (BPOR)
- e-Pro Certification, (e-Pro)
- Resort and Second Home Property Specialist, (RSPS)
- Short Sales and Foreclosure Resource, (SFR)

If your agent has acquired any of these, it is a good start. It shows that they recognize the need for professional development. Note that not all sales skills come from NAR. There are many great sales people who got their sales training in other businesses and now have segued into real estate. They should be more than willing to share with you the name of the sales training they received.

Additionally, there is a vast amount of real estate training available outside of local Boards of Realtors. Obviously, David, too, engages in this kind of training and offers a **Certified Power Marketer**™ PMpro designation to agents as part of his Power Marketing for Luxury Real Estate system in addition to lectures and seminars. Some other names include David Knox seminars, Brian Buffini, Tommy Hopkins, Mike Ferry, Sweathogs, Corcoran Training Seminars, and many more. Look for these names on an agent's resume. Major firms like Coldwell Banker, Century 21, Keller Williams, ReMax and Prudential are often attractive to agents because of their depth of training and support. Look on the agents' resume or personal marketing brochure for any company-sponsored courses they may have taken.

Another indicator of an agent's investing in training can be discerned by asking your agent what professional association meetings they have attended. These include the annual NAR national convention which has over 100 training courses. State Realtor association's annual conventions also offer training. The agent's professional bio should note participation in such events, the seminars attended and courses taken.

Also, ask your agent what sales and marketing books they are reading, what actions they have taken lately to improve their skills including mandatory continuing education courses. Again, what you are doing is not checking their credentials for club membership, but rather their sales and marketing skills. Remember that while knowing someone from the club helps provide both trust and knowledge of their personality and perhaps their ethics, it is still not the whole package. You need someone who can take your listing beyond the club members (most clubs do not want their membership to be used for solicitation purposes anyway). You need someone with sales skills and connectivity beyond such circles.

Besides having this core sales and marketing expertise, agents need additional personal development. Have they taken courses and seminars in time management, web marketing, the latest technical skills, how to deal with different personality types, handling rejection and e-blast marketing?

They also need to demonstrate market expertise. Ask for a copy of their latest Market Report and have them explain to you what is going on in the market. This will help you to determine if they know what they are talking about. Market Reports are often done monthly but we prefer a quarterly one that gives a long-term perspective on the market. A quarterly report helps to smooth out the sometimes erratic monthly swings that market's demonstrate. For a Directory of Market Experts and copies of a Market Report for your local market, go to *http://GetYourHighestPrice.com/Directory.* At this writing, the Directory is growing. If you live in an area not yet covered by an agent-expert on the site, there is a link to invite a good agent to be included by their doing such a Market Report. (Note: listing in the Directory requires payment of a yearly fee and production of a Market Report).

Personal habits

Then there are the personal traits. Do you feel you can get along with the agent you are considering? Are they honest and will they give you honest feedback? Do they seem to have a passion for excellence? A desire to serve? Do they embody good time management? Are they organized, methodical, disciplined, polite, and articulate? Do you like them? Do you feel they listen well, take direction, understand your needs?

"Buying" your listing

Sometimes luxury sellers are impressed with agents who have a lot of expensive listings in their inventory. As a seller you need to know that many agents take a listing at any price, as long as it has the right look (i.e. something that can generate buyer calls) in order to reach several goals. The first is to associate themselves with expensive (but often over-priced) luxury listings to associate their name with the luxury end of the market. They then use these listings to generate high end buyers, knowing full well that those buyers will not likely pay the price of their listings. Instead they take those buyers to more reasonably priced listings and score a sale.

This raises the question of why does the agent you are considering want your listing? The only acceptable reason is because they truly believe they can sell it and earn a commission. But you must beware of agents who pander to you on price (often known as "buying" your listing) just to control the property and use it to get buyers to whom they sell someone else's more accurately priced listing. You may feel good about the price at which they are willing to take the listing, until your property fails to get much activity and you realize you have been used for a different purpose.

Specialization, again

We have already suggested that the most powerful words a listing agent can say to you are, *"I specialize in what you own."* Just as when selling at auction, always hire someone who not only has the above expertise and professional development, but who has taken their skills and focused them on a specific market. The designations we have provided should help, but in addition to them, the agent you are looking to hire may specialize in your subdivision, or in waterfront properties, or large ranches, or sub-divisible property. If you live in a high-rise in a city, they can specialize in just one building. There are agents who handle elderly living, buyer brokerage, and endless other specializations. It is unlikely that there is no specialist for your property's market. Therefore, you should always try to find one, if you can. Their knowledge of the kind of product you are selling and the market for it is among the most valuable assets that an agent has to offer. If you find one who produces a Market Report that covers a product like yours, you will start off way ahead.

About beauty contests

A "beauty contest" is when you invite several agents into your home and ask them to explain why you should hire them. Real estate agents not only accept this competition, they expect it. Therefore do not be shy about interviewing multiple agents for the job. You may need to allocate some time to this, probably as much as two hours for each agent.

We have often been asked whether a seller should engage in a beauty contest if the intention is to list with a friend. We think the answer is 'yes.' Doing so allows you to meet other agents, to see what else is out there, to hear what others are thinking. It even helps you with your friendship because it allows you to emphasize the business relationship and how important this sale is to you.

Preparing to meet the agents

For your first agent meeting and their tour of your property, have ready copies of:

- the plot plan
- survey
- tax map
- tax bill
- deed
- any assessments coming up
- square footage of the house or condo (usually the municipality's field card or assessment document will tell you that)
- written estimates from contractors for work to be done.
- condo, coop or homeowner association documents

The property tour

The first 30 to 45 minutes of your agent meeting should consist of your personally touring the agent around the home. Do not have your caretaker or maid do it. It should be done through your eyes with your commenting about special or important aspects of the property. The tour allows your agent to 'experience' the property through your eyes, emotions, thoughts, and comments.

The agent should be allowed to ask you a lot of questions about it. You, in turn, can gauge whether this particular agent is someone with whom you can connect.

For instance, if you are selling a large land parcel and its essential value lies in its size, but the agent does not want to walk the property lines, you probably have the wrong agent. Similarly, if you are selling a property whose major attribute is a dock for a boat, but the agent is not a boater, there is reasonable doubt that this agent can fully appreciate what you are offering.

Remember, you are looking for someone who can get excited about what you are selling. Enthusiasm sells real estate.

Articulating value

You are also looking for someone who can articulate credible, defensible value for you. Can they deliver your message in a concise elevator speech? The Core Value Calculator we offer agents at our website, *http://PowerMarketing.pro,* provides the calculation easily and the resulting sound bite that interests buyers such as: *"You can purchase this property for 15% (or maybe 20% or 25%) under its Core Value."*

Sitting down with your potential marketer

All the materials you have gathered to review with the agents will help to make them technically proficient in the details of your property (and that is important), but what you are hiring is a marketer, a salesperson. How well they sell themselves to you says a lot about how well they can sell your property.

While you are assessing their sales skills, the agent is simultaneously evaluating you, your motivation and what you have to sell. Each of you should have many questions for the other.

When you sit down with an agent, start by asking if they have any questions for you. Their questions and the ensuing dialogue will tell you a great deal about them. Do not hesitate to provide them your ideas on valuation and how you would defend that valuation to a potential purchaser.

What are the key questions you should have for them? Here are two suggestions: *"How do you position, market and sell properties?"* or *"Do you specialize in what I own?"* These are sufficiently 'wide open questions' (often called Whooopen questions) to get the dialogue started. You are seeking an agent who has some experience with what you own and who knows that the purpose and goal of all marketing is to get you to a moment in time of enjoying multiple buyers bidding simultaneously or the threat thereof.

Yes, you also want specific action steps (color brochures, direct mail, open houses, etc.), but more importantly you want to find out if they know what to do with the buyers produced by such tools. Can they orchestrate markets to get you to that moment in time that achieves the highest price? Agents who tell you all their action steps without first articulating the goal and purpose of those actions usually can't 'see the woods from the trees.'

If you come away from this phase of the beauty contest confident that you have met someone who knows sales and marketing, then you are ready to move on to other aspects of the relationship:

Ask them for:

- Their written Marketing Plan
- Their listing agreement
- For how long they want the listing

Then review with them your own valuation of the property, but allow them to return to present theirs. They will, however, need time to prepare their thoughts, so give them a couple of days. Alternatively, agree to accompany them for an afternoon of driving by and seeing your competition. Plan on sitting down with them to review past sales and do a Core Value calculation to come up with your selling sound-bite.

A Written Marketing Plan

Your agent should be able to produce a written Marketing Plan. The Plan is your agent's promise of what they will do to get your property sold. On your first meeting, they may not yet have such a Plan with them because they must first listen to your goals, understand your needs and view the property before they can create one. But they should represent to you that they will follow up their listing appointment with such a written Marketing Plan. It is, after all, their promise to you and you need to have that promise in writing.

The Marketing Plan will document and lay out their action steps. Know that most agents perform the same "action steps" as other agents. But what distinguishes the agent you want to hire is their knowledge of both the market (do they produce a Market Report?) and their understanding and acceptance of the goal of all the action steps in the Marketing Plan, i.e. to get you to a point in time of having multiple buyers bidding on your property simultaneously or at least produce a credible threat thereof. An agent armed with such market knowledge and marketing expertise makes all the difference in the world.

Many homeowners want the Marketing Plan attached right to the listing agreement and that, too, is wholly appropriate.

A Marketing Services Guarantee

We believe every agent should guarantee their marketing services, but regrettably few do. A Marketing Services Guarantee simply says that they will do what they said they would do in the Marketing Plan. If they do not, you can cancel the listing as long as you have given them at least 72 hours to correct. Some agents fear this idea because they wrongly think that you can cancel the listing if they are unsuccessful in selling your property. But that is not the point. The point of the Guarantee is for your agent to do what they have promised to do in the Marketing Plan. If they have done as promised and your property is not sold, that failure is not a reason in itself to cancel a listing. Failing to do the actions as promised in the Marketing Plan, however, is.

Written Update Letters

Whether you are dealing with a friend or a total stranger, you must establish how often you want to be updated on the progress of the marketing. Much of this is your personal preference. You can be updated after every showing, once a week, by telephone, fax, and email or by a personal visit. "How?" is less important than "When?" You want to be engaged in a dialogue with your listing agent. Before you hire anyone, agree on how and when updates will be handled.

Your agent should agree to provide you periodic written updates. Once a month or every six weeks is a good plan. We suggest such a report be in writing because you will then have a record of everything that has been done on your behalf and it allows you to gauge how well your agent is doing and what is working and what is not. There are always going to be "mid-course corrections" and in order to determine what they should be, you need a thorough update of everything that has been done, what is working and what is not. Armed with that knowledge, you and your agent will be a powerful team determining what has to be done differently to get the job finished.

Meet the office team

When you hire an agent you are also hiring the support team they bring to the sale. Most brokerage firms have a support staff for your agent that includes the receptionist, marketing director, the office manager, personal assistants, the photographer and possibly others. All are part of a team coordinated by your listing agent. A telephone introduction by the listing agent to this team is wholly appropriate. Many details of executing the Marketing Plan will be in the hands of others and you want to know who they are, or at least that they exist.

Alternatively, many top agents work in teams and have a slew of personal assistants or other agents working on their team. Here, too, ask to be introduced to everyone who is working to get your property sold. You should know who they are because you are paying for them.

Some things not to do in choosing an agent

Never choose an agent because you think they may have the buyer. We know how counter-intuitive this seems, but remember you should hire an agent because they have the relationships and reputation to access *all* the buyers in the market, not just one. You should hire them because they know how to use *all* possible means to find *every* buyer, get them all 'in the room' at the same time, raise their comfort level to bid, and then control the psychology of the sale by getting two or more to bid simultaneously. In short, you hire an agent because you have confidence in their marketing skills, not because they have one buyer.

Why you should never ask for a 'quiet' listing.

Almost every real estate agent has faced sellers who do not really want to have their property on the market. Instead, they want a 'quiet' listing, meaning they don't really want all the other agents in town to know they are thinking of selling. They just want an agent to bring them a buyer and they will make a deal. Avoid a quiet listing because:

(1) The news that your property is on the market will get out and be known within hours. The caretaker will tell other caretakers. The maid will tell other maids. A buyer will tell friends who will tell other friends. Somehow it will filter out.

(2) It is not in your interest to have a quiet listing. Review Chapter 3 and the goal of all marketing—multiple buyers, not one.

(3) A "quiet" listing may seem under-handed and even hostile to agents and buyers. Such a closed listing could alienate serious agents and buyers because a seller who wants a quiet listing has, in effect, not accepted the baseline action necessary to sell: putting the property on the market. As a result, agents feel shunted and may talk down your property.

(4) A quiet listing only empowers buyers, not you. Without an organized marketing campaign, the buyers will never feel competition, urgency to act or the comfort to purchase.

(5) When a seller offers a quiet listing, they probably have also offered that same listing to a half a dozen other agents. Instead of agents becoming excited about your listing, they react with a big yawn. *"Oh, they have been trying to sell that quietly for years."* It leads to diminishing the status and importance of the property.

From a marketing point of view, quiet listings usually equate to quiet death. Don't ask for them and flee any agent who agrees to take one.

Discounted commission for an 'in house' sale

Some agencies offer sellers a discount on the commission if their firm produces the buyer. Agencies offer this because it makes you feel good to get a discount when the agency gets to collect a commission on both sides of the sale. We have heard agencies also argue that you should accept this offer because it avoids all the messiness of exposing the property to other agents, does not require you to open up your life to the world via an open house, and can result in a quick sale. Meanwhile, you get a discounted commission, a win-win for all.

While the idea of a slightly discounted commission may be tempting, resist the lure. By accepting this proposition, you have virtually insured that your listing will not be exposed and marketed to all the buyers in the market and therefore you will not get the highest price. Rather, you have incentivized the agency to keep down the outside exposure to score a quick in-house sale and collect the highest commission. Decline such offers.

Give your agent a testimonial, recommendation and referral

After going through this hiring process, we hope you have found a terrific agent. If you have, help to spread the word about them and thereby improve the quality of marketing in the real estate brokerage industry. As in any profession, real estate brokerage needs good agents to be recognized and rewarded. Give a quality agent a recommendation or testimonial so that agent can pass it along to others. Also, like most salespeople, real estate agents work on referrals, meaning one of the most valuable gifts you can give back is to tell another seller about your agent. Hopefully, you feel that their knowledge and skill at getting the highest price makes it easy to give them both a recommendation and a referral. Doing both not only rewards a good agent, but it also helps the next seller and raises the bar for the entire industry.

The Takeaway

- Your listing agent must be a superior salesperson who knows how to sell.

- The agent must have an inclusive mindset and welcome everyone into the sale with a willingness to share the listing with anyone, anywhere, at any time.

- Because your listing agent is your conduit to the agents in the market who have 95% to 100% of the buyers, the agent must have a stellar reputation among other agents. The agent should be trusted, well-liked and be someone with whom others want to work. Testimonials from other agents are telling.

- Your agent should specialize in what you are selling. If not, the agent should at least know how to sell.

- Your listing agent must make selling your property easy for other agents, be hard-working, well-informed, organized, pay attention to small details, return phone calls, willingly and gladly provide information and forms, and be available for showings and negotiations.

- The listing agent's job is not to have the buyer, but to provide you access to ALL the buyers in the market and then know how to use *power marketing* skills to orchestrate them into competitive bidding.

- Your agent should either produce a **Market Report** or have access to one that clearly demonstrates market knowledge. Have them walk you through what the market is doing.

- **The Marketing Plan** is your agent's promise of the detailed actions that will be taken to get the property sold. It should be in writing and can be attached to the listing agreement.

- **A Marketing Services Guarantee**, while not a guarantee of success, is a guarantee that the actions promised in the Marketing Plan will be done. If they are not, the Guarantee should allow you to get out of the listing after giving the agent fair and advance opportunity to take the necessary corrective actions.

- **An Update Letter** serves to provide a written record of all activity on your property and allows you and your agent to review that activity and make mid-course adjustments.

- There should be nothing 'quiet' about your listing.

- **Your Referrals** of quality agents to other sellers not only helps to reward good agents, but also helps the next seller, while raising the bar on the entire real estate brokerage industry.

Chapter 7: Agent marketing tools

Now that you know (1) buyers for your property are most likely to come through other agents, and (2) how to hire an agent who understands what to do with those buyers, this chapter will walk you through the essential tools that are readily available to all agents for finding buyers and making them comfortable to bid. A good Marketing Plan should involve all the following.

Marketing tools: Multiple Listing Service, "MLS"

MLS's are powerful tools and largely do not exist elsewhere in the world, but we are fortunate that the National Association of Realtors™ has spent the last 100 years developing this amazing marketing tool and today virtually every market in the U.S. is covered by one. Of all the tools we will review in this chapter, none are as powerful for finding buyers as your local Multiple Listing Service. Why?

As we indicated earlier many a consumer thinks they should hire an agent based upon an agent's national or international network, or based upon that agent's personal connections in the community, or based upon their "greater than local" reach. But with your listing in the MLS, you get the benefit of all of those networks, all of those connections nationally and internationally and the buyers they produce. (It is your agent, not you, who may want to be with a firm that belongs to such networks so the agent can get more business through referrals and name brand recognition). Instead of worrying about accessing networks, you can focus on something else: an agent's sales and marketing abilities, i.e. on whether they have the *marketing* skills we have articulated here.

Thus, you should be focused on whether they have market knowledge and marketing knowledge instead of worrying about whether you are hiring an agent who can find the buyer. The MLS will largely take care of that. Your focus is to find an agent who knows what to do with those buyers, an agent who can orchestrate them to the single point of time of having multiple buyers bidding simultaneously. The connections you really want are found more efficiently by listing with an agent who is so highly regarded by the brokerage community that you get the benefit of all that community's collective relationships. You want an agent that others enjoy working with so much that those other agents eagerly bring all their buyers to your property.

The only problem with the MLS is that it is so good and so efficient that it actually make agents less sharp. Agents routinely put properties on the MLS and often think there is little else to do but wait for the buyers to arrive. To counter this effect David wrote his **Power Marketing** book, the "bible" for luxury agents. It is why we, together, wrote this book for you, the luxury homeowner. Both books are intent on sharpening an agent's sales and marketing skills by making you aware of what your agent should be doing. The techniques and strategies found here, when combined with the MLS, create the most powerful means of getting you the highest price or the quickest sale.

In sum, what you want in your agent is the skill to know what to do with the buyers that do come through the MLS, and only secondarily

Why go beyond the MLS?

If the MLS is such a powerful a tool, why should an agent do anything else? There are several answers. First, your agent should engage in the following actions in order to find new buyers who have not yet come into the MLS system through another agent. In this way your agent also gets to generate buyers with whom to work. However, please remember what we said earlier: an agent who over-prices your property just to generate buyers is doing you no good. Their over-pricing without a clear, credible and defensible value will only cost you months of time and deprive you of the attention of other agents. Meanwhile it allows your agent to generate buyers and sell them listings that are more accurately and realistically priced than yours. Therefore, while you definitely want your agent to search for buyers, you want them to do so not to sell other properties, but in order to sell yours. Properly pricing your home will allow that to happen.

Nonetheless, despite the fact that you want your agent to find buyers, the chances are very slim that a buyer that calls on one of your ads, or clicks on one of your Internet displays or walks into your open house is going to buy your specific property. Rather, they are likely to buy some other property. After all, this is how buyers come into the hands of agents in the MLS and it is also why the MLS works so efficiently in the marketplace. Just as your agent is generating buyers from your listing who are likely to buy some other listing in the MLS, so too, buyers coming in on other agent's ads may buy your home. The MLS is the vehicle that provides you access to all those buyers.

Second, your agent should do these actions to create the *threat* of finding buyers. Recall *Power Marketing* Mindset # 2 in Chapter 3. That threat also helps to create competition for those coming through the MLS, as we indicated with *Power Marketing* Mindset # 4.

Third, some of the buyers that the agent finds with the following techniques do not even think they are in the market. Neighbors and abutters are good examples. Thus, by engaging in some the following actions, your agent is actually finding or creating buyers and thereby increasing the competition for your property.

Still, while the following tools may find some buyers outside the MLS system, they are also useful for getting the agents in the MLS to bring their buyers to your property. These tools give your property visibility, create "buzz," and raise the comfort level of buyers to act by letting them know there is interest in your property. After all, as you know, everyone wants something more when someone else wants it. Thus, most of the following actions are focused on getting you closer to the goal of creating a competitive environment for your listing or at a minimum the threat of such competition.

Marketing tools: Professional photography

Before a buyer makes a site visit, photographs are the primary means by which someone comes to know your property. Today, professional photography is a more important tool than ever. Agents use the photos in the local and (sometimes) national press, for color brochures, in the MLS, in print ads, for PR and most importantly, on the Internet. Everything buyers initially see, feel, and think about your property is largely controlled by those photographs. Thus, the photos need to be right.

> Everything buyers see, feel, and think about your property is largely controlled by those photographs.

Since professional photography can be expensive, you might want to share in the cost with your agent. You might then keep a set of professional photographs as a nice memento of your home.

Also, if you have old photos of your property, let your listing agent see them. They may be valuable for showing how the property used to look. They also provide a sense of history or nostalgia. Older shots can even be cleverly combined with recent photography, making for a more distinctive brochure.

You probably have a lot to photograph— the house atop the hill with its views of the water, the pool, the entry gates, the main rooms and the guesthouse. Urban agents selling condos or coops may pay slightly less for photography because apartments have less to photograph, however urban properties require skillful interior lighting that can up the cost.

Aerial photographs, especially helicopter shots or cherry picker shots, are often a must for larger properties. However except for the largest ranches, using a small airplane is generally not a good idea for taking photographs. Airplane shots are just too far away and often appear granular.

Importantly, photography should not tell the whole story. The photography is a sales tool, not an archive of the house. But many a luxury seller wants no detail of their property ignored by the camera. This is a mistake. The point of the photographs is to create a mood or emotion that sparks someone's interest. Photographs should tease the buyer into wanting to know more. You don't want a buyer to see in advance every aspect of your property. Therefore, less can often be more. Judicious use of a few select photos can be more effective than an exhaustive tour of every detail of a property.

> The first reaction should be "this is even better than the pictures."

Professional photography is also not about making your house look its best nor making the house look better than it actually is. If the photography is better than the house, then the buyer's first reaction upon seeing the house will be disappointment. You want a buyer's first reaction to be: *"This is even better than the pictures."*

Marketing tools: Broker open houses

Some luxury homeowners prefer to avoid having an open house, viewing the practice as invasive and a violation of their privacy. You should not. The open house is your first live contact with the agents.

Open houses are vital to the marketing process but surprisingly their purpose is not to convey information about your property. Agents will see 10-20 properties on a typical open house day and they are not likely to remember the details of any of them.

Rather, the purpose of the open house is to raise the comfort level of the agents so they will bring their buyers. It is also to control their psychology toward the sale. Thus, the goal is not cerebral or informational, e.g., memorizing the square footage or taxes. Rather, it is visceral. Your agent's job is to create a positive buzz that energizes the brokerage community to want to participate in the sale. In short, the open house should be your property's 'pep rally' orchestrated by your agent as the captain of the cheerleading team.

> The purpose of the open house is to raise the comfort level of the agents so they will bring their buyers.

You might ask: "Isn't this what all agents do at agent open houses?" Sadly, the answer is no. Too often we have walked into open houses with agents distracted by their lap top computers, reading a book, talking with friends, negotiating some other deal and doing everything but cheerleading their listing. Read the story of *Le Domaine Resistance* in Chapter 12 for how an agent open house should be handled.

Opening the house to objections

In addition to being a pep rally, the open house has a second function: it allows your agent to hear and overcome visiting agents' complaints or objections regarding your property. Your agent should ask questions such as, *"What do you think?" "Are there any problems you see?" "What will you say when you present the property to your buyer?"*

While it may seem odd to solicit objections from agents, it is vital and enormously helpful. Agents' objections anticipate what they expect to hear from their buyers. For this reason, you want them to articulate those objections. It is then the listing agent's job to provide them with a response to help sell their buyers on your property. If agents don't voice objections at the open house, your listing agent can't formulate the responses needed. Thus, overcoming and controlling objections is vital to *power marketing's* need to raise the comfort level of buyers.

Never be home

This is why you, the seller, should never be at the open house. Agents simply will not be candid if they know you are lurking around. Go to your health club, get some coffee, go shopping, play golf, but don't be home for the broker open house.

Also, your listing agent should avoid agents speeding through the open house. If possible and if there is any hope of getting a good crowd, your agent might try to schedule the open house on a day when the other agents are not on a caravan tour. Yes, that means that you may not get the property into the market immediately after listing it, but that is fine. Recall, your goal is to find enough buyers to create a competitive situation and get it sold. If that means waiting a few days to get a larger crowd who can spend more time at the property, so be it. Because the agents who come to the open house are likely to have the buyer, don't rush them. Would you want to rush a buyer who had a 95% to 100% chance of buying the property? Think of the agents this way. You want them to spend at least a half hour or longer at the property which they can't really do on caravan.

Also, agent open houses should not be relegated to newbie or other agents. Instead, the listing agent should always be at the open house standing at the door to greet everyone and to say goodbye, providing enthusiasm for the sale. Giving small groups of agents guided tours is also an excellent way to control their psychology toward the sale. Every group should have a guide to take them

> Would you want to rush a buyer who had a 95% to 100% chance of buying the property? Think of the agents this way.

around. This sometimes requires as many as a dozen helpers at a luxury open house. All should be coached on what to say beforehand and each should be thoroughly energized about the sale. Enlisting these helpers means your agent now has important evangelists armed with selling sound-bites who can spread the good news about this property, maybe even sell it to their own buyers. But most emphatically, to repeat an earlier comment, agents should leave with the words they need to sell your home.

Finally, you want agents to take back to their office an excitement about the property generated by your team. Enthusiasm, by the way, sells more real estate than information. In every brokerage community a property either creates a buzz or second thoughts. If agents don't like a property (for any number of reasons), that dislike filters back into the agent opinion pool. Agents who may have never seen the property start to hear negative reports and those reports take on a life of their own. Instead, you want agents to go back to their office and say to fellow agents, "You missed a great one today."

The lingerers

At open houses, the agents who linger the longest sometimes have the fewest buyers. And because these agents seem to have extra time on their hands, they are prone to talk and talk.

Though tiresome and time-consuming, your listing agent should talk to them. You want as many voices as possible talking up your listing, adding to its buzz. By making your open house guests feel like gold, your listing agent is recruiting a formidable force to help promote your property. The fact that the lingerers are talkers can make them valuable mouthpieces for your property, so don't dismiss them too quickly.

Marketing tools: Open houses for neighbors and the client list

Have your agent also hold an open house for the neighbors and for your agent's client list. Don't be disappointed if only a few people show up;

we want any and all of them involved no matter how few come. As we indicated earlier, abutters and neighbors are some of your best prospects. Not only will the neighbors want to know what is going on, but they may know a buyer. Even better, they may be the buyer, since they often have the strongest financial incentive to pay the highest price.

Your agent should send the neighbors a formal invitation or letter with an RSVP (a telephone call or e-mail also works). Why RSVP? You don't want your agent to waste time conducting this open house if no one is coming. Your listing agent should confirm attendance ahead of time. Your agent's letter might read something like this:

Dear Neighbor:

We have been hired by _____ to market the property at _____. As part of our marketing campaign, we like to inform the neighborhood of our efforts. Additionally, we are available to answer questions.

We invite you to a private open house at _____ p.m. on such and such a day. This open house is only for area residents and a proprietary list of potential buyers. If you or someone you know would like to attend, please RSVP at 1-662-LUXURY-0.

Please call the same number if you should have any questions about the property or our marketing efforts.

Sincerely,

Linda and David Michonski
Marketing Consultants
Linda@PowerMarketing.pro
David@PowerMarketing.pro

Neighbors usually attend because (a) they are nosy, (b) they know a potential buyer, or (c) they're interested in buying it themselves.

To enhance neighborhood attendance (recall that you are trying to fill the room) and create an atmosphere of interest in the property, allow your listing agent to supplement the invitation list with a proprietary list of past or current clients and customers. Someone in their past client list may know an interested buyer. Private open houses for neighbors and proprietary lists are akin to a yard sign advertising a property "For Sale." Because such events can be sparsely attended, the invitation must emphasize that it is private. In this way, attendees hopefully come expecting few people. If only one or two people show up, make sure your agent weaves into the conversation that few people were invited and how much you, the seller, wanted only select neighbors invited. You do not want sparse attendance to be interpreted as lack of interest. Rather, turn sparse attendance into exclusiveness.

An open house for a celebrity property is not always possible. But when it is, the celebrity's draw should more than adequately 'fill the room.'

Marketing tools: (first peek) open houses for society agents

Society agents. We all know them. They may do only one sale a year, but it is usually a big or prominent one. Real estate for them is a sideline activity, usually done as a favor for friends at the club. They prospect for buyers at the hair or nail salon, on the beach at Caneel Bay or at the Junior League debutante ball.

While individually they may not sell much, as a group they can sell a good portion of the luxury real estate in upscale communities; therefore, they must be your agent's allies. Have a special open house for both serious luxury agents and the society agents. The event rarely attracts more than twenty to thirty. We recommend your agent make a personal direct call to them that goes something like this:

"I have listed_____and will have a private viewing only for select top luxury agents. I would like you to be one of them."

If your agent serves food at this open house, have them make it special. A couple of bottles of Champagne, some caviar or *foie gras* on a cracker will do the trick. We want this group to feel important and involved and we want to make them allies in controlling what is thought and said about the listing.

On valuables at agent open houses

Sellers often resist an open house because of the presence of valuables in the property. If valuables hinder your agent's ability to sell the property, remove them. The property should not be thought of as Fort Knox. You are trying to sell a piece of real estate, which when sold will be emptied of all such valuables anyway. If they are not enhancing the sale, take them out. If you don't, your agent will spend more time worrying about the valuables than on generating a positive buzz for the property. That, too, defeats the purpose of the open house.

Lock boxes and agent accompaniment

You may wish your agent to accompany buyers on all showings and it is a reasonable request for luxury homeowners to make. For less expensive properties, however, it is not really possible because commissions are lower and the time needed for the many showings is greater. But luxury properties are likely to have far fewer showings due to all the reasons we covered in Chapter 2.

Nonetheless, today's electronic key box system is considered safe because it can tell you exactly what agents have accessed your property, the time of day they entered, how long they stayed, when they exited, etc. You may want to utilize a lock box because it makes showings easier for agents. Usually what makes it easier for agents to show makes it easier for them to sell.

You can still request your agent to be present for initial showings to cheerlead the property. But a lockbox system can facilitate the additional showings required after there is real interest expressed. These showings are often to contractors, decorators, inspectors, etc. The showing procedure should be discussed with your agent and the resulting decision whether the agent should accompany all showings or not will vary widely with local custom and the quality of the local lockbox system.

Marketing tools: Public open houses

Public open houses reduce the prestige of luxury property (at least as we have defined it). For these reasons, avoid them. There are, however, exceptions, including:

- vacant properties, usually those owned by builders (most of the showings will be to curiosity seekers rather than serious buyers, but traffic is important).

- mature estate markets like Beverly Hills, Palm Beach and Greenwich, where the traffic coming in is more likely to be able to afford the properties.

- a gated community where everyone is screened upon entry.

Marketing tools: Arranging property tours for two to four listings

If you live in an exclusive area, your agent should arrange a property tour of three or four other major luxury homes with yours included. This will highlight your property. If yours is clearly the best among them, do not worry about being grouped with inferior listings; the tour allows you to stand out. If you are not the best in the group, then you benefit by being lumped with better properties.

Unlike the broker open house where you must be absent, you should attend this tour in order to view the other properties on it. By doing so, you will come to know your competition and possibly see what the buyers will see when they go house-shopping.

> If you live in an exclusive area, your agent should arrange a property tour of three or four other major estates with yours included.

Marketing tools: The uses and abuses of color brochures

Since luxury marketing was started by Previews in 1933, the color brochure has been a staple marketing tool. For more than seventy-five years, consumers have associated the color brochure with luxury marketing.

The original purpose of these brochures was to lure distant buyers with photos and a description of the property's amenities. For instance, while at Previews, our friend, Jim Retz, handled the sale of movie and TV icon Dean Martin's home in Hidden Valley, California: a sixty-three acre estate with a fourteen-room Spanish Colonial residence and a small golf course, helipad and even bear cages. Upon putting it on the market, he invited agents from the entire West Coast. One agent from San Jose took the four color brochure on a trip to Japan and sold the property to an offshore buyer, sight unseen.

Today brochures have been largely supplanted by the Internet, where buyers can conveniently view multiple pictures and an enormous amount of information about the property.

Nevertheless, we endorse the color brochure as part of luxury marketing. Why?

> Everything we do for buyers in luxury marketing is focused on raising their comfort level in order to induce them to bid freely, eagerly and aggressively.

The Tiffany box effect

Sometimes a buyer's view of something is influenced by how it is wrapped. A beautiful presentation can make a difference. A color brochure:

(1) *makes the buyer feel good.* Everything we do for buyers in luxury marketing is focused on raising their comfort level in order to induce them to bid freely, eagerly and aggressively. The color brochure says, "This is no ordinary property. It is a property for someone extraordinary, like you."

(2) *is a means of communicating from a distance.*
(3) *sets you apart.* Online, every property has six to ten pictures. While being online is critical to providing you the exposure you need, it blurs the distinction among properties. You, however, want to stand out. By sending out a brochure to an interested party, it counteracts the levelling effect of the Internet.
(4) *consistency in message to agents.* By producing a color brochure with all the facts you want known and with even a plot plan reproduced right in the brochure, you and your agent can be assured that everyone in the agent community is getting the same accurate information.

A tool for other agents

Since it's likely that the buyer will come from another agent, the color brochure is also an ideal tool for them to use. We even urge agents to put their company logo on the back of the brochure instead of the front, so that other agents can staple or paste their card over it. Many brokers, especially smaller ones, as in the Sunninghill Farm example (see Chapter 5), will put the color brochure in their windows to glamorize them and lead buyers to think that they handle such upscale properties. Others, like the agent who made the sale of Dean Martin's home, will take them to show buyers. This is exactly what the brochure is for, a tool for other agents to capture buyers' interest.

Lesson: Floor plans

Floor plans are not appropriate for re-sale homes. A simple story demonstrates why. David received about a dozen requests over several months for floor plans on various properties that had been advertised in a national publication. Because all the inquiries came from the same reply address, David grew suspicious and did some research. He learned that the return address was a California state penitentiary.

Direct Mail

The use of direct mail seems to come and go in the real estate brokerage business and today direct mail can be expensive at $.50 per piece or more. On the other hand, the United States Post Office has now initiated a low cost direct mail service called Every Door Direct Mail (EDDM) and it can cost as little as $.14 per piece for the postage. Because it is delivered by mail carrier route, there is no need for a mailing list, nor for creating labels. This has made direct mail much easier and more affordable.

Marketing tools: Just Listed and Just Sold cards

By far the most successful direct mail piece is a Just Listed or Just Sold card or a flyer using the Post Office's new EDDM service. Having your agent send these out to your local upscale market can result in finding a buyer or having the postcard/flyer passed to one. Your listing agent should make sure they convey an upscale image appropriate to the property.

Just to note, the downside to direct mail is not just its cost, but also the fact that at any one time only about 5% to 7% of the population is in the market. Therefore, 93% to 95% of a direct mail campaign is reaching people who are not interested except perhaps out of curiosity. Agents nonetheless will often engage in such direct mail as part of their lead generation efforts and use your listing to get new leads for both buyers and others thinking of selling. Since you get the benefit of the added exposure, let the agent do this kind of direct mail.

Marketing tools: Mailing Color Brochures

In the fall, when Wall Street investment banks and brokerage firms publish their lists of new managing directors or senior vice presidents in the *New York Times* and the *Wall Street Journal*, we cut out the ad and put those names into a database.

We copy the ad, circle the name of the intended recipient with a yellow highlighter and send it to the person mentioned in the ad (who doesn't love to be noticed?). The address of the firms is usually printed at the bottom. We then send each a sampling of our color brochures with a cover letter that reads something like this.

Dear (Rising Star):

Congratulations on your new appointment as Managing Director of _____. Now you deserve something to match your new title and position. Enclosed is a sampling of some of our current inventory. Call to schedule.

With hearty congratulations and best wishes for your continued success,

Sincerely,

David and Linda Michonski
David@PowerMarketing.pro
Linda@PowerMarketing.pro
1-662-LUXURY 0

Your listing agent should watch the local papers for similar advertisements in major industries. After all, these people took out an ad to be noticed, so notice them.

Timing the mailing

These "rising stars" will soon be part of the bonus pool in their firms. Once their names are entered into our database, we find out when bonus day is. Every year, we try to schedule a similar package to arrive within a week of bonuses with a letter like the following:

Dear _____:

Enclosed are a few things to help you make the most of this year's bonus pool. Call to arrange an appointment.
Sincerely,

David and Linda Michonski
Linda@PowerMarketing.pro
David@PowerMarketing.pro
1-662-LUXURY 0

Marketing tools: Virtual tours and videos

Increasingly, the color brochure and print media is being complemented by video marketing. Virtual tours or marketing videos that offer 360-degree views allow someone to get a feel for a room. They provide a sense of walking through a property. When done well, they can be a good sales tool. If your listing agent goes this route, then the rule to follow is the same as for your print photographer: the videographer should take care not to show so much of the property that the buyer has nothing left to call about. The purpose of such videos is the same as all photography: to prompt curiosity and tease the buyer into calling. It is not to satisfy all questions.

Marketing tools: Print advertising

If print advertising sold property, then you could save commission dollars and just hire an advertising company. But the truth is that it doesn't and therefore you shouldn't. At its peak, print advertising was the source of buyer leads only about 14% of the time (at most). Today, the results from print ads are far lower as buyers have moved en masse to the Internet. Overemphasis on print advertising, therefore, is a waste of money and is often done to satisfy the vanity of luxury sellers who like to see their property in magazines. This is therefore called "vanity advertising" and is an unnecessary expense to impose upon your agent. However, if the agent wants to do such ads as image advertising for themselves, then enjoy the benefit, just don't hold out much hope of getting many buyer inquiries.

> Ironically, an ad can be most effective AFTER a buyer has been found or after there is demonstrated interest in a property.

What is the use of print advertising?

If response rates to print advertising of homes is in decline, then does this media still have a place in the agent's tool box? We think it does, but for a different reason than it seems. Most luxury homeowners think a print ad is for the purpose of finding a buyer. But as we have already indicated, 95% to 100% of the buyers will come from other agents, not ads. Ironically, therefore, an ad can be most effective not to find a buyer, but rather AFTER a buyer has already been found or after there is demonstrated interest in a property.

The reason for this is that an ad can pose a threat to a buyer and thereby create buyer urgency to act. If, for instance, a buyer has made an offer on a property and your listing agent is trying to get them up in price or create some competition, then your listing agent might inform the buyer's agent that an ad will appear in such and such a publication. Once informed, we can virtually guarantee that the buyer will buy that publication and look to see the ad. Its presence creates the threat of loss and thus creates pressure to act. Recall from prior chapters that fear of loss is an emotion we want ever-present in the negotiations. Advertising can help to promote it.

The second use of advertising comes right at the beginning of a listing, but its purpose is less to advertise to buyers than to call agents' attention to the property. For the few buyers reading the print ads your listing may be something new that they have not seen before. Therefore, while it may prompt them to call their agent for a showing, more often it is the agents who read the ads diligently and are reminded to call their buyers. Ironically, therefore, print ads advertise more to agents and result in more agent calls than buyer calls.

Marketing tools: The Internet

Today, the consumer, both million dollar and mass market, is on the Internet. This includes Silicon Valley techies, venture capitalists, hedge fund managers, Wall Street investment bankers or couples going online after the kids have gone to bed.

> Properties must be on as many heavily trafficked sites as possible.

Most are surfing websites like _www.Realtor.com._ The consumer no longer takes several days off to meet an agent, get in a car, and start scurrying around neighborhoods to find a home. Consumers today pre-qualify properties via the photos, descriptions and virtual tours on real estate listing websites.

Given your desire for the widest and broadest exposure possible, that means your property must be on as many heavily trafficked sites as possible. While the sites come and go, the Internet is here to stay. It is the Internet, not a specific website that is the magic bullet. Your listing should be where the action is: on these heavily trafficked websites as well as those focused on luxury properties.

Marketing tools: International

While there have been some attempts to create an international MLS, the core of MLS philosophy is the willingness to share listings. But sharing or co-brokering listings is not common outside the US, even where there are mature markets like Ireland and England. The emphasis is often on smaller commissions and selling a property directly. The 5 percent to 6 percent commission that prevails throughout most of the United States is rarely found elsewhere. As a result, the incentive to offer co-brokerage or to pay a referral fee is less. This hinders the ability to create the commission-sharing arrangements at the heart of an international MLS. Thus, while the superstructure for making international referrals is in place via the International Consortium of Real Estate Associations ("ICREA" founded in 2000), still low commissions in other countries crimp the flow of referrals. Fortunately, in the United States sellers pay higher commissions which allow American agents to pay referral fees to non-American agents. If in the future the dollar falls and America goes on sale, this fact will be very important in attracting foreign buyers.

Currently, we recommend two sites: _www.Realtor.com_ which is now accepting international listings and ICREA's website, _www.WorldProperties.com_ with listings currently from 30+ countries. Your listing should be on both and on any international franchise or network sites, if your agent is part of one.

Marketing tools: E-blasts

Today, e-blasts are an inexpensive way for agents to keep a property in front of the local (and non-local) brokerage community and to provide regular updates on its marketing. Once the list of other agents is set up (which may take some time), your agent can communicate with this group on short notice. When you are engaged in serious negotiations with several buyers, e-blasts are an excellent way for your agent to communicate that there is real activity on your property and that, if anyone has buyers, they should bring them now or forever hold their peace. E-blasts can be made to the entire MLS or to as many luxury agents as your listing agent has gathered.

Marketing by Association

Earlier we mentioned bundling your luxury property into a broker tour with other luxury listings. Marketing the property by association with other upscale products is also a way to call attention to the property and reassure buyers that your listing is associated with comparable luxury products, brands and events. Some events to consider are:

Have an important artist or prestigious art gallery hold a "by invitation only" opening for their artwork in the property.

Sponsor a trunk show of boutique designer-type clothes that brings in upscale buyers.

Host or allow your agent to host a charity event that attracts a high-end clientele.

Schedule an antique car show to be held on the grounds of the estate.

If it is a waterfront property with sufficient dockage or mooring area, host an antique boat show.

Designer show houses are also a possibility, but often require a property to be off the market for up to a year.

Marketing tools: Publicity before the sale

Publicity can be gold because it sets your property apart and gives it a little celebrity value and thereby increases the buyers' comfort level with the property. Let's deal with the two variables.

First, you must consent to publicity. If you are a very private person, this may be difficult for you. However, if yours is a celebrity property, or a property that is going to get media attention anyway (it may have some renown, have been the site for a movie shoot, or have some local historical importance), accept that media attention, however unwanted, will arrive at your door. You need to be prepared for it. Accept that you are going to be put in the public eye, even though you may not want the attention. Thus, if less media attention is your goal, then pre-empt it by having your agent do something counter-intuitive, such as issue a press release and even hold a press conference. Your agent can influence what is said by suggesting alternate stories or points of interest about the property.

If you want more media attention

On the other hand, if you do not mind some media attention or actually encourage it, your agent should engage in proactive promotion. Surprisingly, this is often pretty mundane stuff such as:

"123 Jackson Road came on the market this week at a price of $9.2M. The property, formerly the home of our town founders is now owned by Mr. and Mrs. Kendal Rogers who descended from town founder, Ermile Jackson. The sale is being handled by Ken Smith of Famous Properties."

That is it. Sometimes by just giving the facts straightaway, you avoid all the unwanted baggage that can get added to a story.

If you want publicity, but there is not much to say about your property, you and your listing agent will have to get creative. You have to find something that would lend itself to a story about the property. Usually this can revolve around you, for example:

"Such and such estate is the home of _____, who is one of the owners of ...."

Stories can also revolve around architecture, history, size, unusual events that occurred, etc. You will need to sit down with your agent's PR brain trust and together try to figure out an angle to promote the property.

Hiring a professional publicist is often the way to go, especially if you are not good at handling the press. This is an expense that you should pick up. After all, the publicity is a consequence of who you are or the property you own. The publicity is likely to benefit you either by promoting the property or protecting you. Either way, it should be your cost.

If you are a celebrity or CEO, you probably have a publicist. You or your agent need to sit down with them so everyone knows the story line in advance.

Marketing tools: Publicity after the sale

Publicity after the sale usually involves the press wanting to know the selling price. Disclose it. It is public information and will get out eventually, so why not control it?

The press will also want to know who the buyer is. Hiding it can generate intense media attention that may be the opposite of what you want. Better to just tell them and get it over with.

The press also will want to know what the buyer is going to do with the property. You can dismiss the question by simply saying "That has not been determined" or "We don't know" or "We have no comment on that."

Marketing tools: Making the Last Call to get buyers

Throughout this book, we have emphasized the Last Call as your agent's most powerful marketing action. We all know that at an auction when the gavel threatens to come down, bidders acquire an urgency to act. This is the tool that gets you the highest price possible—sometimes a record price. But not only does it move existing buyers, it deserves a place in this chapter as an important tool to find additional or new buyers. Here is what happens when the Last Call is made:

- The called agents will tell the agents sitting next to them that there is a lot of action on your property.

- The called agents, in turn, now have a new reason to call their buyers.

- The agents sitting around the called agent may over-hear the discussion and be reminded to show it to their buyers.

- Those who have already passed on the property, now decide that, given the action, maybe they should give it another peek, if just to make sure it isn't for them. This adds to last minute traffic and the number of showings and helps to keep the room filled.

- The called agents may now have new buyers and add your property to their showing list.

Reminder: making the Last Call also means calling the property's neighbors and abutters again. Give the abutters one final chance to step up and buy. After all, they may have the most to lose from missing the sale or the most to gain from buying the property.

The Takeaway

1. The **Multiple Listing Service** must always be used because through it, 95% to 100% of the buyers are likely to come. All of the following tools are meant to enhance

your property among the agents in the MLS or help to create the threat of competition for the buyers they will bring.

2. **Photography** must always be high quality, designed to interest and lure, but photography should never tell the whole story or look better than the property itself.

3. **Agent open houses** should be used positively to affect the psychology of a sale from the very start. They are pep rallies led by your listing agent as the captain of your property's cheerleading squad.

4. **Private open houses** for neighbors and client lists can (1) generate buzz, (2) provide buyers from the neighbors who want someone they know to make the purchase or, (3) stimulate interest from the attendees themselves.

5. **First peek open houses** for society agents and serious luxury agents help to garner key opinion leaders behind the sale and control a positive psychology.

6. **Lockboxes** help to increase showings by making it easier for agents. Today, the security issues have largely been solved.

7. **Public open houses** for luxury property (as we have defined it) risk attracting curiosity-seekers and with the exception of vacant builder homes, gated communities and very rich towns, they are best avoided.

8. **Agent tours** of two to four listings may yield buyers, position your property favorably, and serve as a reality check for you.

9. **Color brochures** are one of the oldest and best marketing materials. They can enhance the image of your property and set it apart.

10. **Direct mail** pieces such as personal letters at bonus time and Just Listed and Just Sold cards are ideal for targeting an audience.

11. **Virtual tours or videography** should follow the same principle as all photography; tease to get a call, but don't show everything.

12. **Print advertising's** primary value has diminished substantially, but it may still be effective to force action right at the beginning of a listing or *after* a buyer has expressed interest.

13. **The Internet** should be extensively used to promote listings on as many high traffic websites as possible.

14. **International buyers** will come through local agents' connections, their membership in international networking sites and through your property being listed on *www.Realtor.com, www.WorldProperties.com,* major franchise websites and international networks.

15. **E-mail blasts** allow for low-cost exposure to agents and easy Last Call updates.

16. **Associated or Affiliated Marketing** allows the property to be marketed in association with high end events such as charities.

17. **Public Relations** is highly effective for increasing the property's stature, even possibly giving it a little celebrity

value. When you sell, tell the media your name as the seller, the price the property sold for and what the buyer will do with the property.

18. The **Last Call** not only can energize existing buyers to act, but it can also result in finding new buyers.

Chapter 8: Qualifying Buyers

Agents sometime argue that they do not want to share their luxury listings with agents outside the local upscale community because those agents are not luxury agents and, thus, are not likely to have qualified buyers.

This argument engages in clairvoyance: how do they know in advance that other agents won't have a buyer? What if we had not offered Sunninghill Farm to that "shabby chic" one–woman office? Worse, it belies an unwillingness to qualify buyers. Not taking this step results in limiting the market for your property. Qualifying is your agent's job. It is not up to the selling or co-broking agents to qualify their customers for your property (although they should, if only not to waste their own time). Rather, it is emphatically your listing agent's job to qualify every buyer.

Luxury property marketing requires more qualification of buyers than ordinary marketing

While all agents should be welcomed to your luxury listing, you cannot just allow anyone to view it. After all, you may have expensive antiques, art work or other valuables in your property. Thus, your listing agent will have to spend more time qualifying the pool of buyers and separating out those who can afford to buy from those who cannot. It requires more than putting a key box on a listing and letting co-brokers bring anyone and everyone into it.

Types of Buyers: "Location specific" vs. "Property specific"

We like to begin qualifying by asking whether a buyer is *"location specific"* or *"property specific."*

Most buyers are "location specific." They want to be in this town and this area and then within a specific price range. On the other hand, a "property specific" buyer does not care where the property is located as long as it has certain characteristics. This may mean having an in-law suite or accommodation for a 92-foot yacht. The buyer may be searching for a five thousand to one hundred thousand acre ranch and not care whether it is in Montana, Wyoming or Colorado. Or, she may be interested only in mountain or ocean views or insist on being right on a lake. This is a "property specific" buyer.

Therefore, agents should begin the qualifying process by asking buyers:

- Are they "property specific" or "location specific?"

- What else have the buyers seen?

- What did they like or dislike about each property?

- Why did they not buy it? (The answer will often give a very good idea of their interest level.)

- How long have they been looking?

- What is their timetable for purchase?

Be aware that the "property specific" buyer may have been looking a long time. In their case, the length of time looking is not always an indication of a lack of urgency to buy. The property they are seeking could be in any number of locations, and it takes time to check out so many sites.

Other qualifying tips

- Be warned that if the buyer is a "one in a million" buyer, meaning they are looking for something highly specific, they will know how few buyers share their specialized interest and most assuredly will need a reason to pay up. You now know what it is: credible and defensible discounted value clearly demonstrated combined with orchestrated competition by your agent (or the threat thereof).

- Sometimes new buyers come into the market only because a special property is now available. Because such buyers usually have highly specialized desires, they may have less to choose from and be more concerned about real or threatened competition. This means they are also more motivated to pay up. Presenting potential competition to them is, therefore, effective.

- Qualifying by your listing agent also includes talking with the agent who is representing the buyer. We like to know how long the agent has worked with the buyer. The amount of time invested gives an indication of how serious the agent thinks this buyer is. We ask candidly, "Are your people serious?" As agents, we like to hear why the other agent thinks the buyer is worth their time.

- Even though wealthy people are notoriously private, you should make clear that you will not allow a showing without financial qualification or at least personal identification. Therefore, either you must know the person, or you must know that she currently lives in, say, an $11M house and can afford this one. Your agent can call her company, her advisers and intermediaries (as with the buyer for Sunninghill) to confirm the information. If the individual is part of a public company, your agent can go to their website for their latest annual report.

To financially qualify buyers:

- Get references from the buyer's financial advisers, banker, lawyer, etc.

- If they are taking out a mortgage, have your agent talk to their mortgage broker and get a pre-qualification letter indicating that they are qualified to buy and for how much.

- Call their company to confirm who they are. Check the 10K, annual report, or other public reports.

- Check their website or Google them.

- Use social networks such as LinkedIn or Facebook.

Information is more public today than ever before and there is more of it. Therefore, personal identification is easy. Indeed, today the red flag is when there is no information. Under such circumstances, it is fine to go back to the buyer and ask for background information. If unwilling to provide it, ask for some references. If not provided, beware.

The problem of international buyers

Confidentiality issues multiply in the case of foreign buyers. In some cultures, hiding wealth is an ever-present passion; in others, it is considered vulgar to talk about it or display it. International buyers also feel that by giving up their financial information they are giving up key negotiating leverage, so they are reluctant to do it.

Your agent must insist that no showings to international buyers can take place unless they are qualified. Even if they cannot get financial information on the foreign purchaser, they can at least get references. None is more critical than the buyer's banker. Any foreign buyer must have a banker here in the US who will handle their fund transfers. If they do not have one yet, they are probably not ready to buy. They should also have a good immigration attorney for all the residency issues surrounding a foreign purchase. If they do not have one, they also are probably not ready to buy.

Your listing agent should be prepared to ask these questions of foreign buyers:

- Have you ever bought in the US? If so, where?

- Why are you looking to make this purchase?

- What is your timetable?

- How long have you been looking?

Many such questions, however, will need to be asked obliquely rather than directly; this is an art form in itself.[9]

With foreign purchasers you need to worry less about security issues and more about time wasted. If a foreign customer must see a property by such and such a time because they are leaving the country in a day, they are probably not going to buy. Without the time to truly consider an international purchase, they will likely lose the urge to buy as soon as they land back in their home country. If they have been here for a week and they call on your property the last day, they probably are just tired of being a tourist and have decided to go see some nice real estate. You don't want to play that game.

The Takeaway

- **Categorize Buyers** by determining their type as *location specific* or *property specific* buyers.

- **Qualify Buyers** through their bankers, mortgage brokers, lawyers, investment advisers, their agent and other intermediaries.

- **Qualify International Buyers** as you would US buyers. The international market is still emerging and difficult to access. But if you get a foreign buyer, make sure they have their banking and immigration advisers in place.

Chapter 9:
Business essentials of a luxury listing contract

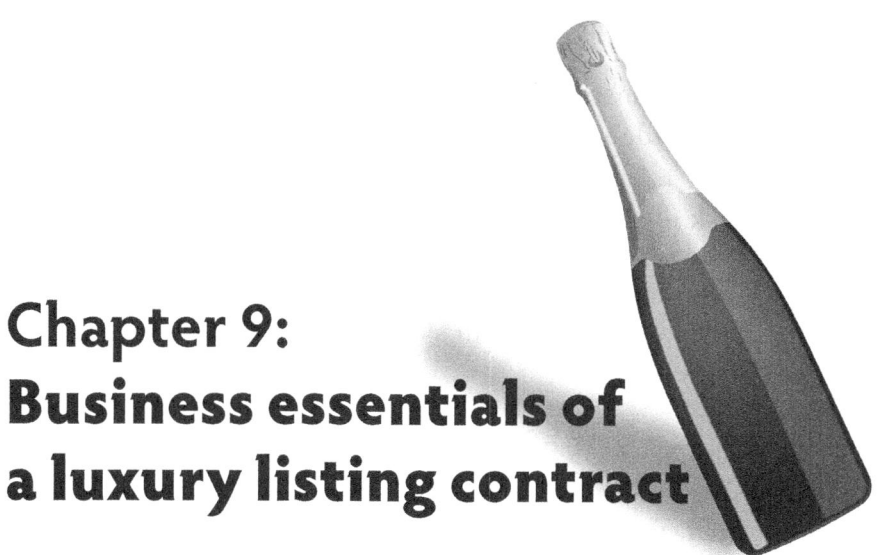

In order to get your property into the market with an agent, we recommend that you list it via an exclusive right to sell contract. These listing contracts vary with state laws and local MLS customs, but some essential business principles should be in every such contract. In this section, we will briefly go through those business points.

About risk

As a seller listing a major asset, you are married to the agent you choose for the term of the agreement. By accepting the listing that agent is equally bound to you. While you are putting up a valuable asset for sale and paying a substantial commission (as we argue later you should), the agent is wagering their time and money on you for 12 months or more. Both of you are at risk. The listing contract should be designed to reduce some of that risk and create a fair balance between both sides.

Chapter 2 demonstrated the small size of the luxury market and the inherent formidable risks. Those risks include:

- The risk of your property becoming stale from being on the market too long. This can be due to the fact that most luxury properties take at least twelve to sixteen months to sell (in reasonably good markets). In slow markets, they can easily take 24-36 months.

- The risk associated with spending more money. Your agent will spend more money on marketing a luxury property, most of which will be spent up front in the initial two or three months of the listing.

- The risk of more work for your agent from the longer time on market. Your agent will spend more time being present for showings, updating you for a longer time, coordinating with your accountant, lawyer, trust officers, investment adviser, public relations people, etc. Since you, too, are probably busy, you know that time is money and you each will risk a lot of both.

- The risk of your time inconvenience. Because the property will be on the market longer, you will have a longer period of inconvenience from keeping the house neat and tidy and preparing for showings. You will also have the stress issues that come from opening your life to the world.

Be unafraid to talk about it

As a luxury property owner you are probably a solid business person who did not get where you are by needlessly risking your money or time. You understand risk and reward and therefore should talk about it openly with your agent. Haphazard negotiations over the listing agreement often foreshadow problems down the line. Whenever we see a listing agreement that offers weak protection for the homeowner or the agent, disaster for both usually looms not too far ahead. Why? Because if a fundamentally unfair deal has been struck, it can lead to either bitterness between the parties or less than a zealous effort by the agent. You don't want either.

Involve attorneys

Far too often, sellers and agents see the attorney as necessary only at the end of the process, more for clean-up than for strategy or negotiating. This is a mistake. Lawyers should be brought in at the beginning of the process, preferably during the listing contract negotiation. You may hesitate, not wanting the legal meter running, but it will prevent expensive and time-consuming problems from surfacing during the marketing, bidding and sales process.

13 business essentials of a good luxury listing contract

1. ENABLING CLAUSES

Usually listing agreements begin with the granting or "enabling" clause under which you (the owner) grant to the broker the exclusive right to sell the property. The listing agreement will state that you are authorizing (or enabling) your agent to offer the property at the listed price, which normally will be some dollar amount payable in cash or other terms acceptable to you. This section also deals with terms and effective date(s).

Additionally, these clauses enable brokers to use sub-agents or buyer brokers, advertise, create brochures, hold open houses, put up signs, use the MLS, list the property on the Internet, and so on. This is all somewhat boilerplate.

2. REFERRING ALL INQUIRIES TO YOUR AGENT

One clause to note: an exclusive right to sell listing agreement means you must refer all inquiries or offers concerning the listed property to your agent.

This sentence provides an important protection for the agent and a critical incentive that must be in place to keep an agent loyal, focused and enthusiastic about selling your property. It also gets to the heart of an exclusive right to sell listing. It is what differentiates it from an exclusive agency listing (which we strongly discourage agents from ever taking).

This clause says that even if a neighbor or friend contacts you, you must refer them to your agent. This is important to the agent for the reason above, but it is also important to you. Your agent cannot do their job of orchestrating all the bidders if you and another party are holding side negotiations. Imagine the chaos if done at an auction. Sidebars also could prompt buyers to walk away because they feel such sidebars violate the fairness of the process integral to raising buyers' comfort.

3. PAYING A COMMISSION, WHEN AND ON WHAT TERMS

Because agents work on incentives, it is important to make sure the incentives are clear and everyone knows how much they are going to be paid, under what circumstances, and when.

The agreement should have a clause that says, if during the term of the listing contract, the listed property is sold or the broker or anyone else (including but not limited to a buyer's broker) finds a buyer ready, willing, and able to buy the listed property on the terms specified in your listing contract or on any other terms acceptable to you, you agree that the broker has earned their commission when the contract is signed and all contingencies in it have been met. The broker is then due some percent of the agreed upon sales price to be paid at time of closing or at time of default, whichever comes sooner.

As discussed in Chapter 4, listing prices are meant to generate interest and provide a target for buyers. They also provide a target or goal for your agent. This clause provides that goal. However, this can be slightly problematic if you list the property for a low, attractive price in order to spur offers above the asking price. In this case (i.e. when you want to under-price your property in order to rapidly fill the room and create competition), the phraseology can be changed to your owing a commission when you sign a contract for any price acceptable to you. While we prefer a clear target to hit, if the target is set low to attract a plethora of buyers, we gladly will revert to being paid upon your obtaining any price acceptable to you and forego a targeted higher goal.

Whether your agent is paid upon hitting a specified goal or upon exceeding a low goal in an amount acceptable to you, this part of the listing agreement gets to the heart of a commission business. Salespeople need to know that they will get paid when they hit a goal, especially if, as is most often the case with luxury asking prices, the goal is an aggressive one. For an additional discussion about incentive commissions, see Chapter 11.

Some attorneys argue that the agent's job is not finished when a contract is signed and all contingencies have been met. Rather, they argue that the agent should only be paid if, as and when title actually closes. If the property does not close, no commission is paid.

We disagree with such a clause because it presumes (1) it was the agent's fault that the sale didn't close, or (2) that the agent could have prevented the sale from not closing, or (3) that the seller gains no benefit from the sale not closing. But it is possible that none of these presumptions are true; that it was not the agent's fault that it didn't close, that the agent could not have prevented it and the seller could get a windfall benefit by retaining the 10% deposit.

Let's recall that the agent's job is first to do whatever you hired them to do. For example let's say the job is to get you $3,950,000 cash with no contingencies and close within 60 days of signing the contract. If you hire someone to do a job and they do it, shouldn't they be paid? Second, if they don't do what you originally set out, but they do something that is completely acceptable to you and you sign a contract agreeing to it, then when all the contingencies have been met, haven't they done what you hired them to do? Recall that their original job was to create and orchestrate a market for your property that yields the highest price acceptable to you, then get the buyer to sign a contract that at some point is free of contingencies. We believe at that point, the agent has done their job. You have a non-contingent contract for a price you willingly accepted. The agent is entitled to their commission. If there is a default by either the buyer or by you, then the default clauses kick in (see below) and cover that eventuality.

What the above argument by some attorneys means is that even if you willingly default on the contract, the agent is not paid. Further, it says that if the buyer defaults and you keep a 10% deposit, the agent gets nothing because there was no closing. We believe this is unfair to the agent. It also does you a disservice because it diminishes the incentives for the agent and their brokerage firm to give you the highest attention and, quite obviously, that is the opposite of what you want.

Set the terms

Because we believe an agent should be paid for doing what you hire them to do, it is imperative that you are crystal clear on what that is. This includes not just the price you are seeking, but also all the terms of sale. They should be set forth clearly in the listing agreement. For example, your agent may bring in a full price offer, but it might require 100 percent seller financing or a one-year closing or it may include other terms unacceptable to you.

To deal with this, just put in the listing agreement under "terms" any that are appropriate. For instance, you could write: "Terms: cash, no contingencies, closing within 60 days or less."

What is important is clarity. Because brokerage is an incentive business, work with the agent and your attorney to make clear exactly under what circumstance or terms the agent will be paid, when and how much commission is due.

4. BUYER DEFAULT CLAUSE

The Buyer Default Clause states that should the buyer default in the performance of the contract you split the deposit with your agent.

Because of a buyer default, you are going to get as much as a 10 percent windfall and since both you and your agent have been inconvenienced by the default (and disappointed to lose the buyer), that deposit is split 50/50. In some states this is just a matter of state law. In others it is open for negotiation.

½ of the deposit versus ½ of the retained deposit

You may wish to insert that you will only split any "retained" deposits. We go along with this argument with a little foot-dragging because if you don't retain the deposit, we are sympathetic to your having to go into your own pocket to pay us. But we "foot-drag" because as agents we want you to have an incentive to retain the defaulted deposit. Remember if the agent agrees to compensation only on "retained" deposits, then if you do not retain the deposit, no one gets anything except the buyer, who gets back their money while simultaneously being the cause of the default They win; you and your agent lose.

While we urge you to go along with what is both customary and often state law, as indicated above, at an absolute minimum we believe you owe your agent a commission on whatever you get as a retained deposit under a default, i.e. if the agreed upon commission is 6%, then your agent should minimally get 6% times the 10% deposit. This means that if the default amount on, say, a $3,000,000 sale is $300,000, then, at a minimum, your agent should get the commission times that amount, or $18,000.

Failed sale	=	$3,000,000
Default amount	=	$300,000 (10 %)
Multiplied by the commission	=	6 %
Minimum payment	=	$18,000

If your agent is willing to accept this minimal amount, we recommend you give them something back in the form of an extension of the listing for a period equal to the time between signing the contract and the date of default. At least in this way, your agent is being given more time on their listing to try to recoup their time and financial investment in marketing your property. There are three possible default clauses we use, depending on the situation.

(1) *"Should the Buyer default in the performance of the contract, the agent will be entitled, in lieu of commission, to no more than one-half of any deposits given by the Buyer."*

Or, if you have the right not to retain the deposit, we recommend using this one.

(2) *"Should the Buyer default in the performance of the contract, the agent will be entitled, in lieu of commission, to no more than one-half of any deposits given by the Buyer and retained by the seller and this listing contract will be extended for a period of time from date of contract to the date of default."*

Or, if the agent is willing to agree to be paid a commission on only the defaulted amount:

(3) *"Should the Buyer default in the performance of the contract, the agent will be entitled to the percentage of agreed upon commission times any deposits given by the Buyer and retained by the seller and this listing contract will be extended for a period of time from date of contract to the date of default."*

5. *OWNER DEFAULT CLAUSE*

Next, you must address what happens if you default. A typical default clause says that should you default in the performance of the contract, then the commission is earned (based on the contract price), due, and payable in full at the time of such default. We believe that if your agent has done their job, found you an acceptable buyer, and then you default on the contract, you owe them their full commission. After all, they did the job for which you hired them. Pay them.

6. WITHDRAWAL CLAUSE

A withdrawal clause deals with the possibility that your circumstances may change and you want to withdraw the property from the market. In most mass-market transactions, agents routinely grant this as a courtesy. But given the amount of money and time spent on a luxury property, it can be a significant problem in luxury real estate marketing. We try to have any withdrawal discussion revolve around two principles:

Principle #1: You should be able to withdraw your property listing from the market at any time, but if you do so, the broker must be compensated at least for out of pocket expenses and time invested.

Principle #2: You cannot then sell the property yourself or through another broker during the period of the original listing agreement. If you do, you owe at least the listing side of the commission.

To address Principle # 1, the clause we like states that, should you withdraw this property from the market before the listing expiration date, then you will pay the broker, within 30 days of such action, all documented marketing expenses to include photography, brochure preparation and production, mailings, advertising, and other promotional expenses specific to the property *and* a fee of 1 percent of the listed price in consideration for the time and overhead associated with having marketed the property.

To address Principal #2 above, we add that a withdrawal *"shall not be construed as releasing you, the owner(s), from any other provisions of this agreement."* What does this mean?

No release

It means that even after a withdrawal, the exclusive is still in full force and you are liable for a commission if a sale occurs. Thus, the clause allows you to withdraw the property, but you cannot then sell it through another broker or sell it to your friend or neighbor without paying the agent. This is an important sentence for your agent because an owner could lie about their reasons for withdrawal to save a commission and then turn around and try to sell the property themselves. Therefore, if you are trying to sell the property privately and circumvent paying a commission, your listing agent is protected for at least the listing side of the commission. If you have bona fide reasons to withdraw, you can do so by paying only the amounts negotiated in Principle #1, but you cannot then sell the property yourself.

If you die

Sometimes we have encountered the following objection: What if an owner dies and their heirs decide not to sell the house? Why should the heirs be penalized by having to pay a withdrawal feel equal to the agent's expenses plus 1%, all for something beyond their control?

Our first response is this: if they should not be penalized for circumstances outside their control, why should your agent? If you hire a contractor to put a new addition onto your house and you die, should the contractor fail to be paid? What about the contractor's loss of revenue from working on this job instead of working on another? What about his time investment and out of pocket expenses that were incurred? Is he to absorb the loss? Like a contractor, your agent needs compensation for the time and money invested.

In addition, the heirs should be reminded that your wishes were to sell the house. If it is the choice of the heirs not to comply with your wishes, why should your agent be penalized for their decision?

A question of quality

The most valid rationale for your withdrawal has nothing to do with external circumstances, but is based on poor performance by your agent. If you are not sure of your agent, then don't hire them. Check out their letters of reference, their testimonials. Interview them more than once. Go over their Marketing Plan and Listing Agreement completely. Your agent will not mind. Good agents want you to be sure about them and they want to be sure about you. The more time you allocate checking each other out, the better the subsequent marriage will work.

In sum, if the situation is not the extreme of death, but rather that you might want to change your mind about selling, then have a frank discussion with your agent before you list about the chances of this happening. As a professional who is risking time and money for the next 12 to 18 months, your agent should know what circumstances would prompt you to withdraw. Your agent can then evaluate the risk of such a withdrawal and decide accordingly.

7. *REASONABLE LEGAL FEES*

This clause means that if you have to be sued to collect a commission, you pay the legal tab. You should not have any trouble with this clause unless you really do not intend to pay, in which case don't hire an agent.

8. *PROTECTION CLAUSE*

Your agent will want a clause that says if the property is purchased by any buyers who saw it during the term of the listing contract, the agent gets a commission. Our clause reads as follows:

"This Agreement will expire on_____. Notwithstanding such expiration, we are entitled to a commission if within twelve months after such date the Owner(s) sells the property or any portion thereof (1) to any Buyer with whom negotiations were pending at the time of such expiration, or (2) to any Buyer to whom the Property was shown by us or any other broker through whom we marketed the Property. We will submit a list to the Owner(s) of all known protected buyers under (1) and (2) above within fourteen days of the expiration of the listing agreement."

This clause is especially necessary in luxury listing contracts due to the diminished urgency of luxury buyers to act. They get easily distracted with handling a new corporate merger or producing a new film or something else. Buying their dream home can often take a back seat to more pressing business. While this book is geared to getting reluctant buyers to act, nonetheless, a buyer who views the property during its initial week on the market may come back months or even a year later to buy. Your agent needs to protect themselves against this eventuality. After all, you hired the agent to find buyers; if they find them while they are the listing agent, don't penalize them if the buyer purchases the day after the listing expires.

Seasoned agents know that buyers can often sense a listing expiration on the horizon. Such buyers may delay their negotiations in the hope that, after the listing expires, they can get the property without a commission. This makes sense. Every buyer wants to get the best deal. But if they are waiting for the listing to expire, they want to save more than the commission. With the competition from the market gone, they are likely to negotiate down a price much lower than the commission amount.

It is also true that agents who neglect to include the protection clause tend toward panic about sixty days before their listing expires and pressure buyers to make an offer. The subliminal message is "Hurry and buy this home because my listing is expiring." Buyers can sense a squeeze coming and may withdraw altogether and await the listing to expire. A protection clause, however, allows your agent to stay focused on the best means of eliciting offers and hastening a sale. We know that agents' fiduciary responsibilities should be enough to make sure their professionalism rules, but we always think that in an incentive business, the incentives should align with the desired actions. Having such a clause allows your agent's professionalism to remain intact and you will be better served.

> With the competition from the market gone, they will negotiate down a price much lower than the commission amount.

Only rarely have we encountered problems with a protection clause from an attorney. The principal point of debate usually centers on how long the agent should have. We think 12 months is fair, can settle for nine, but no less than six. We worked hard for all those buyers and, if finding them results in a sale, we deserve a commission.

The protection clause also serves another purpose: protecting other agents. Because of this clause, we can protect them for a commission six to twelve months after the listing expires. This raises their comfort level to bring buyers at any time. The protection clause assures them they will get paid if they have shown the property and registered their buyer with us. This kind of clause is particularly important thirty to sixty days before an expiration, as the other agents feel a high comfort level in still bringing their buyer to the listing, knowing they are protected after it expires.

Hopefully, all of this is moot and upon expiration of the listing, you are so enamored with your agent that you can frankly discuss any problems, review the marketing campaign, create a plan of correction (if necessary), re-list the property and reach your goal.

9. LEASE CLAUSE

Whenever we work a resort or second home market, we find owners eager to rent their home for the seasonal months, as rentals, especially luxury rentals, can fetch hefty prices. Often after listing their property—usually in the doldrums of the off season—they inform us that they have secured an irresistible rental. They assure us not to worry because the tenants will allow the property to be shown on twenty-four hour notice.

A renter in a property can be an agent's nightmare, not only because the casualness of the vacation season makes it difficult to keep a property looking its best, but also because buyers in a resort area often expect immediate showings. They will drop into a local broker's office on one of their vacation afternoons and want to see a property right then. The renters, however, who are responsible for how the property looks, are, after all, on vacation. That means they often leave an untidy house. Even after giving the tenant twenty-four hour notice, it's not uncommon to find snorkels in the hall, wet towels on the floor, trash fermenting in the kitchen or last night's pizza still on the counter. This poor showing reduces the chances of a sale. Thus, even with a twenty-four hour notice built into the lease, renters are a problem for selling a home.

If you live in a resort area or a location where there is a high likelihood of renting your property, you should put a clause into the listing agreement that, while allowing you to lease, also protects your agent against any interruption of marketing that such leasing may cause. This clause extends the period of the listing by a time equivalent to the term of any lease. Our clause reads as follows:

"Should the Owner(s) lease the Listed Property for any time during the above listing period, this agreement will be automatically extended for a period equal to the term of the lease."

If, for instance, you rent out your property from Memorial Day to Labor Day, this clause would extend the listing for three months. Similarly, if you took a ski property off the market for a Christmas to March 30 rental, it would extend the listing for 3 ½ months.

10. THOSE THAT COME AFTER

If you die, the listing agreement should not die with you. *You* chose this agent and *you* agreed to this agreement. Therefore, it stands to reason that *your* heirs and executors should respect *your* decision. If estate taxes are an issue, then you do not want your death to interrupt the marketing process as getting the property sold may take on even greater importance. We use a clause like this:

"This Agreement shall be binding upon and inure to the benefit of the respective executors, administrators, heirs, successors and assigns of the parties...."

This clause also protects the agent against your assigning the property to others, willingly or unwillingly. If, for instance, you go into bankruptcy, the property may then be assigned to a bankruptcy estate and be administrated by a bankruptcy trustee. Meanwhile, your agent can then continue trying to sell it for the bankruptcy estate.

11. WARRANTY CLAUSE

The warranty clause simply says that you warrant title to be marketable and you have the right to sell the property. The clause should force you to be sure that all is fine with the title before marketing commences, rather than after. Our clause reads:

"The undersigned warrants they are the sole owner of the property, title is marketable, and they have the right to sell the property."

In deed

Reading your deed should be a part of preparation for selling. Pull out a copy and read it. It can be fun, especially with older deeds in rural areas. You'll be able to recognize red flag items such as easements, exclusions, mineral rights, rights of way, imprecise boundary descriptions and alert your agent to them. Make sure you give a copy of the deed to the agent to read, too. Four eyes are better than two.

12. EXCLUSION CLAUSE

Sometimes you may know a buyer and want to exclude them from the listing agreement. By now, you know that you cannot get the highest price for your property without creating a competitive situation. And you cannot induce competition if you have several sidebars going on with various buyers. Thus, such exclusions give the excluded buyer a preferential position in the negotiations and because they are outside the agent's agreement, it is like the auctioneer trying to sell your property in one room while you are trying to sell it in a side room. The fundamental fairness of the whole process is also undermined. Buyers get discouraged (not to mention your agent). Much of the momentum needed to get the property sold dissipates or vanishes altogether. Avoid such clauses.

> Use the threat of listing the property with a real estate agent to create an urgency to act..

How to get the exclusion you want

Nonetheless, there is a way to avoid the negative marketing message exclusions create, still get the exclusion you want and maybe even stimulate the whole marketing process. First, use the threat of listing the property with a real estate agent to create an urgency to act on the part of the interested buyer. You do this by listing the property with your agent and then putting the would-be buyers on an excluded list. Tell them that if they can act within, say, a two-week window, they can get the property for slightly less because you will be able to save on commission. *The key is to exclude them only for a period that really should not exceed two weeks.* By narrowing the window of time within which the excluded buyers must conclude a deal, while offering them a slight discount, you force them to put their chips on the table. You create an urgency to act. This allows your agent two weeks to focus on getting the property photographed, creating the brochure, placing the ads, getting the copy ready for the MLS, etc., while you try to cut a deal with the buyer.

Be forewarned, however, it is highly unlikely this buyer will act. Why? Because even though they may want the property, their desire has not been validated by the desire of other buyers and, therefore, they will be slow to act, if at all.

> Their desire has not been validated by the desire of other buyers.

If we are correct, you will not likely get anything out of them until your agent's listing contract kicks in after 14 days and your excluded buyers feel the pressure of the marketing campaign and the validation from your agent's "filling the room" with other buyers. If so, it will be your agent's marketing effort, not the exclusion, that gets them to the table and the exclusion comes off. If your agent can put a deal together, your agent has now done what you hired them to do. They took all buyers, including yours, and got them to your goal. Congratulate your agent and pay them. Remember, it is not important who finds the buyer. What is important is that you have a listing agent who can orchestrate all of them to that point in time of having several buyers, or the threat thereof, bidding simultaneously. Only this gets you the highest price.

13. GET A LAWYER CLAUSE

Our clause is pretty boilerplate text:

"This is a legally binding contract. If not understood, seek competent legal advice."

Length of the listing

You and your agent will have to agree on the term of the listing agreement. The agent should be able to get from the local MLS the average time on market for selling properties in your price range. Once known, that should be the minimal listing time. Why would you want to give the agent less?

Attaching the Marketing Plan

You may wish to include the Marketing Plan as part of the legal agreement. Since your agent created the Marketing Plan and intends to do everything in it, she should have no problem agreeing to incorporate it. You may also want your agent to screen the financial capability of all buyers and there is no problem stating that in the listing agreement, too.

Review the entire listing agreement

You now know the essential business points that should be in every luxury listing agreement. Most of these agreements are boiler plate. Others are more customized. Whatever the firm's agreement, go over it line by line with the agent. It is important for you to know what obligations you both are incurring.

The Takeaway

- Spend time with your agent to create a listing contract that provides incentives needed to overcome the additional risks of marketing luxury real estate and gets you to the goal of selling this property for the highest price.

- Involve any attorneys from the beginning so they feel part of the overall team and your agent feels comfortable talking to them.

- Set the terms and clauses appropriate to both your and the agent's time/money investment.

- Meet head-on the issues related to a buyer or owner default and withdrawals (with the appropriate deposits, fees due and other issues). There is no substitute for honest, straightforward discussion.

- Dispense with buyer exclusions because they undermine competition; but if you insist, force your buyers into acting within a narrow time frame of no more than 14 days.

- Marketing Plans are fine to attach to listing agreements and you should openly discuss with your agent the pros and cons of lock boxes and listing-agent-accompanied showings.

- Review every line of the contract with your agent. Similarly, read and share all deeds and other related documents.

Chapter 10: For Sale by Owner (FSBO)

If we were to say that under no circumstances should you try to sell your luxury property by yourself and become a For Sale by Owner (FSBO), you may think we are trying to protect our turf. If so, then consider the following facts.

We have shown how small the market is for your property; how the key to getting the few smart luxury buyers to act is to present them with competition. That competition increases their anxiety about losing the property while simultaneously raising their comfort level to buy by validating their buying decision. Your agent must then orchestrate everyone to one competitive moment in time of multiple buyers bidding simultaneously. In short, to get the highest price you need to create and then orchestrate competition.

Knowing that statistically there is better than a 95% (more likely 100%) chance that the buyer is sitting out in the brokerage community (and today probably has an exclusive right to represent contract with a buyer agent), why bet on the slim odds that you can do this yourself? Why deny yourself access to 95% (and possibly 100%) of the buyers who are sitting in the hands of the agents? Why deny yourself access to those agents by failing to be in the MLS? Further, why take the personal risk of having strangers come to your house? Or, why deny yourself the agent's ability to make the Last Call, especially since we have already demonstrated that making the Last Call can pay the commission and may even net you an extra 10% or 20% or even 30%?

National Association of Realtors® studies have found that the longer your property is on the market the greater the risk it has of becoming stale.[10] Be certain to read about "stepladder marketing" in Chapter 12, Listings that explain it all, *Le Domaine Résistance*. It illustrates the danger of having a stale listing and the herculean effort needed to refresh it and get smart buyers to bid.

Understand that we could not agree more with your desire to maximize the amount of money you net from the sale of one of your largest assets. That is, after all, why we wrote this book: to get you the highest price. What concerns us is your possibly using the FSBO tool to reach that goal. If we really thought you could make more money by selling your property yourself, we would have written that book instead. But the fact is that we can't because the likelihood of success is slim, the disadvantages are daunting and not worth the risks. The chances are also high that you will end up paying a commission, but net less than if you started with a good agent.

By now, this book should have helped you to understand the expertise and skill needed to sell a luxury home. We also hope you understand that advertising does not sell real estate and open houses are not simple exercises. Instead, they are highly coordinated tools to positively and energetically influence how the brokerage community views your property. We hope that we have convinced you that you do not need one buyer in a million, but at least two, or the perception or threat of two, or more. We also hope you understand that buyers will have objections to your property and your agent must listen to them, and prepare and deliver answers to those objections. Your agent must also control the psychology of the sale, creating the comfort necessary to prompt action and overcome a lack of urgency to act. Now you know that it is one thing to secure a buyer and it is another to be able to skillfully orchestrate a competitive situation that results in a purchase.

Why become a FSBO?

Having warned you of the risks, let's review some of the most common reasons why you may still be considering going the FSBO route.

- Properties are selling quickly and you believe you don't need an agent.
- You believe selling your property will be easy.
- You think you will net a higher price by saving a commission.
- You have the time to do your own marketing, showing, and negotiating.
- You always wanted to be a real estate agent.
- You think you may know the buyer and believe that you can cut a deal with them. The potential buyer may be a neighbor or friend who once expressed an interest in the property or you think the buyer is likely to belong to your club or association or is involved in the charities you support, etc.[11]
- You don't feel you know a competent agent who can handle your luxury property.
- You don't like real estate agents.

Helping you (to do something you should not do)

If, because of any of these reasons, you insist on going the FSBO route, you will need the following:

- Advice on how to get your home ready for sale.
- Tips on staging your property.
- Tips on how to show the property.
- Information on lead paint disclosure from HUD.
- Other property disclosure forms (unless you are selling "as is").
- Likely inspections, such as a home, termite and radon.

- All condominium or cooperative documents and HOA or coop board application forms.
- A seller net sheet to calculate what you will realize from the sale; a similar sheet for the buyers on how much they need to bring to the closing.
- How to expose your property through advertising, discount brokerage firms and websites such as *http://ForSaleByOwner.com*.
- Suggestions for print ads, signs, sign-in sheets, etc.
- A mechanism to qualify buyers.
- A blank HUD Settlement Sheet.
- Information on mortgage financing.
- School reports for the buyers, if applicable.

But remember these points:

- You are denying yourself access to where the buyers are (in the brokerage community).

- You are left without professional marketing expertise that can create a market and the necessary urgency for buyers to act.

- To sell your property your primary lures are discount pricing to create good value and lots of costly and ineffective advertising.

- You have almost a nine out of ten chance that you will end up using an agent anyway, pay a commission, and probably get a lower price because the property's prime marketing period was wasted.

- Owners, who sell through a real estate professional, sell their home for 15 percent more than people who sell their homes themselves.[12]

If you still wish to be a FSBO and are willing to under-price your property to sell it, then go to one of the many discount brokerage firms that for a flat fee provide some of the services you will need. For example, for six hundred dollars a firm in Utah will give you a yard sign, a listing on the company's website and on the MLS, all the forms you will need, a booklet on selling and marketing, and all disclosure forms. For an additional 1 percent of the sale price, an agent will write the offer, review the documentation and attend the closing. What you do not get is pricing guidance, advertising, caravan tour attention (when agents go on tour to view properties) and perhaps most importantly, a practitioner's brain to pick and with whom to strategize, let alone orchestrate any offers and the sale.

Even if you use a discount firm to get your property on the MLS, you may still expose yourself to a commission for the buyer-broker, requiring you to pay at least half of what you would traditionally pay. You could pay more than half, too. When a buyer-agent sees that your property is listed with a discounter, they sometimes expect a higher commission because they are doing double the work. As a consequence, you may end up increasing the amount of commission from 2.5 percent up to 3.5 percent, 4 percent, or higher. In sum, discount brokerages provide you some of the forms, processes, and procedures you need, but they provide none of the expertise that is required for *power marketing,* and they may end up costing you almost as much as a traditional brokerage firm.

Seller beware

As a FSBO, not only are you likely to get a lower price, but you may not even save any commission at all. Why? Because buyers know all about real estate commissions and they automatically assume that because you are selling yourself, they can discount your price by the amount of the commission. Therefore, only the buyer, not you, saves a commission on the sale.

Because it is highly unlikely that you can orchestrate multiple buyers all bidding simultaneously, your buyers will lack urgency. Be aware also that by attempting to sell your property yourself, you are exposing yourself to buyers who are smart, sophisticated and intelligent, and who will use your lack of professional representation and the resulting lack of competition to get a bargain for themselves.

The Takeaway

- Because FSBO listings stay on the market longer, involve greater inconvenience and safety issues and rely on discounting to attract buyers, they result in either a lower sales price or eventually listing with an agent.

Chapter 11: Paying a higher commission and why you might

Agents work on commission. They sell what they get paid to sell. To get the highest price, you have to incentivize them. If you pay them well, they get excited. If you don't pay them well, they work for those who do.

If you think this chapter is an attempt to convince you to pay a higher commission, you are right. Over and over we have learned that we all get what we pay for. The real estate brokerage business is no different.

We have already stated that a real estate listing agent should be an essential member of your financial team. But unlike most team members who bill hourly or get a percentage of assets under management, real estate agents daily put themselves at risk for their time and money. While they are "on call" (and often work) seven days a week, they only get paid upon success. Because your agent's commission is not fixed, but negotiable, it can go down, but it can also go up. This chapter is about why you may want to pay more.

Determining the commission to be paid

How much should you pay in commission? While local practices will differ, our rule of thumb is to ask around for what is the going rate and then always pay more. The commission you are paying has two parts: the amount paid to the agent you hire to sell your property, known as the listing agent, and the amount paid to the agent who produces the buyer. The agent with the buyer is called the selling agent (sometimes also known as the "buyer-agent" or the "co-operating agent" or the "co-broker"). They will share in the total commission and in most states the amount paid to them is first determined by you and written into the listing contract.

To determine how much to pay each, first decide how much you are going to pay to the selling agent. Your listing agent may start by asking you this question, too, because that agent must indicate the amount in the listing agreement and in the Multiple Listing Service.

Again, in our view, the answer is simple. If the market is slow and lots of properties are on the market with few buyers, you want the attention of all agents. If you determine that the going rate paid to selling agents is 2.5%, pay them 3%, or, if the going rate is 3%, pay them 3.5%. Whatever the going rate is, increase it. You want to send a strong message to buyer's agents that you want to sell, you are willing to pay, and you are not at odds with the real estate brokerage community. Also, be welcoming to agents. Agents like to be welcomed, not shunned. Wouldn't you?

A story about how agents think

While this book was in its final edits, a situation arose that so clearly demonstrated why you might want to pay more that we had to include it. We were asked to do a book signing for the *Power Marketing* book at a friend's open house in Manhattan, New York. He was selling a $4.3M penthouse apartment on East 72 Street. The apartment was wonderful with 1800 square feet of outdoor space combined with 2600 square feet indoors. Despite it's being one of the only apartments in such a prime area with so much expansive outdoor space, for some reason the property had not attracted many agents and there were few showings. "Filling the room" for this apartment had become difficult.

At the open house we talked to agents about what needed to be done. One agent who had a super sales record claimed it was $1M overpriced and if it were "marked down" it would get some action. We talked at length about pricing with her because given what else was available, it seemed to us fairly priced.

Then this agent changed course and lobbed another objection, now saying it was a "gut rehab." When we asked her how much she thought it needed, she indicated $500,000 to $1,000,000. The broad and highly inexact figure caused us to doubt and debate the renovation amount (read a similar story in *Le Domaine Résistance* in Chapter 12). It seemed like the typical "wave your arms" estimates that agents often throw around. Worse, we thought the apartment was in terrific shape, as no doubt did the seller.

Then, this agent turned from objections to providing a positive recommendation: raise the commission for the selling agent from 3% to 5%. That, she assured us, would solve everything. Given that she thought it was $1M overpriced and then that it needed $1M of work, we were stunned by how quickly she felt both objections would disappear if the commission were raised. We asked somewhat incredulously, was raising the selling commission to 5% going to solve those problems? Yes, she assured us. Pay the agents enough and they'll sell anything. Welcome to how many agents think.

Do we need to say more?

Some MLS systems in the United States can even be searched by size of commission. For instance, when an agent does a search and comes up with 10 properties to show a buyer, some systems allow the agent to rank the properties based upon the commission being paid. You want to be on top of that list.

This is a perfectly rational exercise. If you were working on commission, wouldn't you want to know which seller is paying you more to get their job done? The buyer agent may have to disclose to their buyer that they are getting paid more to sell your listing (state laws and customs vary on this point), but so what? The point is to get the buyer agent's attention and attract showings.

The listing agent's commission

Next, you must determine how much to pay the listing agent. If the listing agent is the person who gave you this book, that agent has probably already embraced its lessons. How much is this marketing expertise worth to you? If you agree that a good agent is a value-added marketing consultant, then the commission should be in line with the benefit and the value-added dollars created. The agent who gave you this book may be the agent who can work most effectively with you because they probably share the mindset needed to get the highest price.

The rarity of *power marketing* agents

An agent's expertise at *power marketing*, when combined with their knowledge of the local real estate market, makes them a "leading authority" on selling property in your market. Why? Although there are over three million licensed agents (over one million belong to the National Association of Realtors®), the number who understand the lessons of this book are as few as the luxury homes under our "2-3 x average price" definition. Because at this writing *power marketing* is not well known and not widely practiced, a *power marketing* agent is a true rarity.

We suggest the same rule as above: find out what the going rate is and pay more. The goal is to reward someone who has taken the time to truly understand how to get you the highest price.

What about special bonuses?

In determining incentives, steer away from special bonuses, i.e. a cruise or weekend at your ski house. Why? First, the agent's firm cannot usually share in this bonus. Therefore, the firm has no additional incentive to focus more on your listing. Second, it can get cumbersome to offer a reward. For instance, if you are rewarding the selling agent (the one with the buyer), what happens if they work with a partner? Are you giving two bonuses? What if the buyer, as often happens, was a referral from another agent? Are you giving each a trip? Figuring this out is too complicated. Keep incentives simple. Better to just pay a little extra commission to everyone and be done with it.

> A highly effective incentive is something that attracts agents to your open house.

Nonetheless, a highly effective incentive is something that attracts agents to your open house. As we have described earlier, your listing agent's first task is to "fill the room" with as many buyers as possible, and, since those buyers are sitting in the hands of the agents in your community, it means attracting agents to the open houses. Holding a raffle or giving away a dinner at a local restaurant increases your attendance. Want a line out the door of your property on open house day? Offer a three day cruise to someone who attends and puts their card in a raffle. That will get everyone to focus on your property's open house.

Additionally, if your listing agent schedules the open house at a time different from your market's normal open house days (sometimes known as "caravans"), a little incentive to get agents focused on coming to your event is worth the cost.

Luxury marketing costs more

If the idea of paying more to sell a luxury property is hard to swallow, just remember that it costs more to sell a luxury home. Whereas, the cost of selling any home includes an MLS listing fee, a sign, Internet and other publicizing, the cost of selling a luxury property is higher. Image advertising in prestigious magazines often runs in the thousands of dollars per page. Open houses, photography, and brochures can quickly rack up thousands of dollars in up-front expenses. Additionally, video imaging and stand-alone websites for individual properties can add cost. Other ancillary costs include quality business cards, listing and promotional material, stationery. The list goes on. There is also the cost to your agent in time for having to be present for every showing. That takes time away from their other activities and time is money.

Finally, good agents want to be housed in good firms with solid support services. This often involves rent for a prime, high traffic location in town with ample parking, pleasant offices and room for support staff. Like all top producers in any field, they need the support of a good manager, a marketing department, IT staff, design and production people, a public relations department, and often a good personal assistant. This means that whatever you pay the agent, it is split with their firm and perhaps again with their personal assistant. If your listing agent is taking home half of the listing side of the commission (half of half the commission) before taxes and expenses, they are usually doing quite well. Normally, after taxes and expenses, they are netting about 1/4 to 1/8 of the total commission, far less than most people imagine.

Listing time is longer

Because the luxury market is characterized by sellers who do not have to sell and buyers who do not have to buy (with the resulting lack of urgency to act), it takes longer to sell a luxury property. This means that the minimum listing period needs to be for one year and often eighteen months and occasionally even two years. To determine a fair listing time period, have your agent verify the average listing time for luxury properties in your market and then use that as the minimum length of your agreement. If it will take an average of eighteen months to sell a property, then that should be your listing time.

After reading our materials, your agent should be able to sell a luxury property in less time than average. Perhaps our work can help to reduce time on market, but for now list for no less than the average period it takes to sell a luxury property in your market.

Paying for quality

In short, the few agents who can articulate and achieve the goal of all luxury *power marketing*—multiple buyers bidding simultaneously or the threat thereof—deserve generous commissions. Recall in Chapter 4 the story of how a client got almost 25 percent more by Linda making a series of Last Calls. In the next chapter, read the story of *Le Domaine Resistance* and how "stepladder marketing" resulted in the sale at full price of a property that had been on the market for eight years. In Chapter 13 read how making the Last Call for Clarendon Court added $250,000 extra to the price and resulted in its sale for $2M more than any other property had ever sold in that market. Are not such results worth a generous or at least a full commission?

The Takeaway

- Agents are commission-based. They work harder for higher commissions.

- Pay more than most everyone else.

- Focus special incentives on getting agents to the open houses.

- *Power Marketing* agents are more likely to achieve a higher price and thereby provide value greater than their commission.

Chapter 12: Sales that explain it all - Le Domaine Résistance

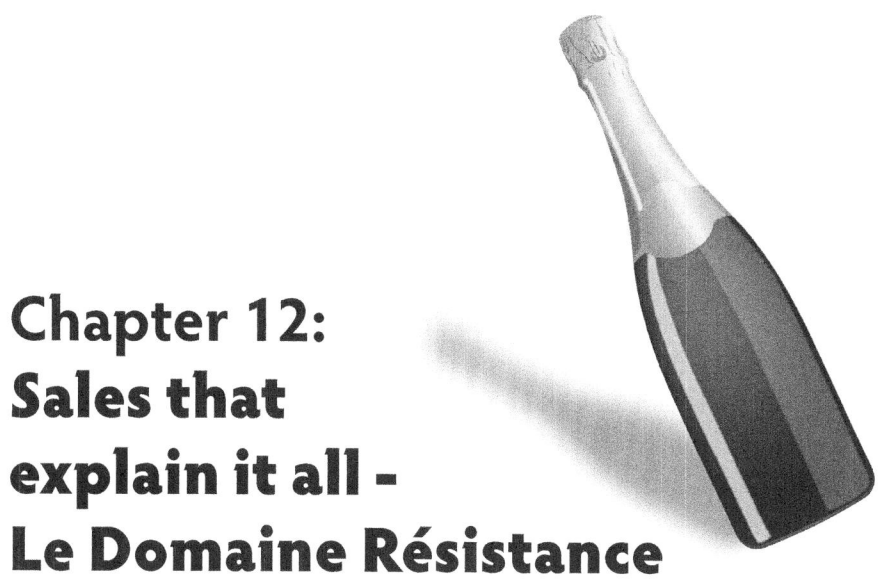

I t's story time.

David's first story

Le Domaine Résistance is a fictitious name for a real property. I have changed the names of those involved to keep the focus on the marketing principles and away from the characters and personalities.

How do you sell a magnificent luxury estate that has been on the market for eight years without an offer? The answer has everything to do with luxury *power marketing*. This story is about orchestrating local agents and local buyers to create competition and raise comfort using nothing more exotic than the Multiple Listing Service.

My goal: to create a market for a property that had been entombed in the ennui of agents and their buyers. How? By raising and orchestrating everyone's comfort level to act, excitement was resuscitated and un-froze the local buyers who now felt able and willing to bid. Once a market that previously did not exist was created, 14 offers were generated and the property sold for full price.

By way of background, at the time of this listing my former firm (LandVest) worked on an "affiliate" system under which local agents brought us hard to sell properties and we charged a premium commission to get the job done, boasting a 93% track record of success. In this case our affiliate was a firm named Douglas Elliman on the North Shore of Long Island, New York. We had never listed a property in that market and we were searching for one that would help to establish our reputation. That meant the seller was going to have all the stops pulled out to get their property sold because, by our selling it, we were also establishing a track record and a beachhead for future sales.

Because we represented a different, non-local means of selling expensive properties, it was not surprising that when I was invited to address the Douglas Elliman sales meeting in its Locust Valley office one Tuesday, the able manager, Louise O'Rourke, introduced me enthusiastically as a new resource for properties over $1.2M (today it would be over $3.5M). The manager told the agents that now, when they had a challenging luxury listing lead, they could bring me in to help.

One agent, Helen Woodbridge, jumped up from her desk with great enthusiasm and yelled across the sales meeting: *"I have the perfect property."*[14] Louise asked which one. Helen gave an impish if not mischievous smile and said, *"Le Domaine Résistance, of course."* Everyone in the room laughed and applauded Helen for her suggestion.

When I asked why it was such a good candidate, I learned that the property had been on the market for eight years without any offers. There was great laughter. From her office, Helen produced the original listing form from eight years earlier.

"You see, David, no one can sell Le Domaine Résistance." Helen explained that every firm in town had been given the listing at one

time or another, but never to any avail and that now, given the length of time it had been on the market, *Le Domaine Résistance* gave new meaning to the term "a stale property."

> "You see, David, no one can sell Le Domaine Résistance."

Helen's suggestion utterly delighted the room of agents. The many nodding heads seemed to agree that this was, indeed, the listing on which I could cut my teeth. Their facial expressions and body language said, *"Yeah, give him that listing. That'll test his skills. We'll be able to see how good he is."* Or, as one broker shouted out, *"If you can sell that property, you can sell anything."*

Having the right look

Before I accepted this challenge, I asked to see some pictures of the property. When I saw them, I was elated. *Le Domaine Résistance* had an imposing gate attached to square brick pillars, flanked by two gate houses. Once through the gate, a winding drive went up a gentle hill that sheltered the house from the main road and ended in a courtyard. It was clearly a magnificent estate set on five acres. It was what we called a "signature" or "statement" property. No one could possibly drive into this estate and not be impressed, even before the main door was opened.

The listing price in 1985 was $995,000, $200,000 below our minimum listing at the time (adjusted for values today it would be over $3,000,000). We took a year listing at a 10 percent commission with no up-front fee.

The first thing we did was have it photographed to create a stunning four-page, color brochure. The brochure was mailed out with an announcement to the brokerage community inviting their cooperation in the sale and offering a full 3 percent selling fee to anyone with a buyer.

Getting the inside scoop

We received dozens of calls from agents. Some wanted to know who we were and what we were doing in their market. Others called to inform us of the property's sorry listing history. Some called to tell us there had never been an offer because the property needed five hundred thousand dollars of work. Someone else called to say it needed seven hundred thousand and another agent estimated the work at around a million dollars. Still others called to say we were wasting our time and the seller was not serious.

This feedback made clear the two initial jobs. The first was to get some accuracy on how much work the place needed, knowing that every buyer would exaggerate the amount of work and use it as leverage for getting a lower price. It became clear that over the years, the issue had escalated. Buyers threw out ever higher estimates that were repeated by unknowing agents. We knew that whenever we had a wild spread of numbers such as five hundred thousand to a million, greater accuracy was required. Most importantly, to establish a positive psychology to the sale, agents had to know what the repairs might cost. Only then could we start trying to convince them that there was hope for a deal.

The second job was to change the psychology of this listing from that of an un-saleable stale property to one that would definitely be sold. We had to overcome the belief of many agents that it was a waste of their time to deal with any seller who would allow a property to be on the market for eight years.

Estimating the cost of work to be done

We collaborated with Helen Woodbridge to bring a small army of contractors into the property. Pointing was necessary on the exterior brick. The driveway needed some patching and new pebbles laid down. One of the brick perimeter walls had cracked and was leaning. The paint on the gates was peeling. Several fieldstones around the pool were cracked. Inside, the parquet floors needed refinishing, and two rooms needed some re-plastering and repainting where a prior leak had bubbled and stained the wall. The kitchen needed some updating and the addition of modern appliances. Some door handles needed tightening or outright replacement. The circular stairs in the turret creaked.

Every repair was documented with written estimates. Sometimes, if we thought the estimates were too high, we got a second or a third opinion. At the end of a process lasting about two weeks, we had a 'to do' list and we sat down with our client and presented it. We informed her that the extent of the repairs had become an issue that was affecting the reputation of the property and that we had to bring clarity and accuracy to the discussion. She was delighted that we had taken the time to quantify the work being done, but when presented with the $125,000 to $150,000 price estimate, she politely refused to do any of the work.

> We had quantified the amount of repairs and could use written estimates that would help put the seller in a stronger position to counteract the negotiating leverage the repairs gave the buyers.

We were disappointed that she would not even consider doing the two least expensive and most impressionable repairs: scraping and repainting the front entry gates and re-plastering and repainting certain walls.

But we had to sell this property. At least now we had quantified the amount of repairs and could use written estimates that would help put the seller in a stronger position to counteract the negotiating leverage the repairs gave the buyers. We also had established that the repairs were nowhere near the five hundred thousand to one million dollars that had been bandied about. By having this all researched, we countered this objection before it was made.

Making new friends

There was more work for us to do. We needed to enlist allies in the effort to control the sales psychology. Not only did we want every agent to feel welcomed into the sale, but we called every agent who inquired to thank them for taking an interest in the property. We also invited those who called to a special private preview of the property two hours before the first broker open house. We said that we expected a large turnout and wanted to meet them beforehand to personally thank each and then provide a private tour.

Anyone inquiring about the repairs (or expressing an opinion about the extent of them) was told that they had come in at around $125,000, based on written estimates provided by half a dozen contractors and we would be happy to provide them to the agent or to their buyers.

Agent ennui

Almost everyone gave us the agent response typical for when a property has been on the market too long. They told us that they had already seen the property many times. They alerted us that there had been many broker open houses over the years and there was really no reason to see it again. It was a lovely property, they politely said, but the time on market had taught them that the seller was not serious. Thank you, but it was a waste of their time—and ours, too, in case we wanted to know.

Our response was to thank them again for their candor and proceed to an objection handling technique known as reflective listening.

"I know how you feel. I felt the same way when I first learned of the

> It was a lovely property but the time on market had taught them that the seller was not serious. Thank you, but it was a waste of their time—and ours, too, in case we wanted to know.

> "I'd like to meet you so that when you have a buyer, we know each other. That way we can make this deal happen."

property. But having met with the seller, I am confident that there is going to be a sale here. We sell 93 percent of the properties we list and this property is going to be sold, too."

"Since it is going to be sold, we'd love you to be the selling agent who gets the full 3 percent commission."

"Will you indulge me for one more trip to the property, not so much to see it, but to meet me? I'd like to meet you so that when you have a buyer, we know each other. That way we can make this deal happen. What do you say? Would you join me at noon at the property?"

Most agents agreed. To the few who resisted, I said:

"If you can sell a property that no one else has been able to sell in eight years, imagine how your reputation will soar. Picture how much business you will receive. Come and meet me so that we can get this job done together. What do you say?"

More than one hundred agents came, many because they had heard from the several dozen with whom I had spoken personally that they should check out "this guy who thinks he can sell *Le Domaine Résistance*." I was glad to have them.

We had prepared a little booklet about the repairs. We wanted this issue totally defused by straight talk so that we could center the discussions on what *had* to be done as opposed to what someone *might* want to do.

> We noted the sum total for all the repairs and then listed them. In the back were the estimates. It was a complete package that every agent could instantly give to any buyer.

On the first page of the booklet we noted the sum total for all the repairs and then listed each individually. In the back were the estimates. It was a complete package that an agent could instantly give to a buyer who thought the property needed too much work. Thus, we had made it easy for the agents to overcome any objection to the repairs.

Getting the market over its weariness

The first victory was getting agents to attend the open house. We could never control the psychology of the sale without meeting them. We had to look them in the eye, defuse the issue of the needed work and impart confidence that a sale would happen. Thinking in terms of our auction analogy, we had filled the room, at least with agents.

> "Will you help me to get this sale done?"

The day of the open house I stood at the door, having memorized the names of each of the two dozen or so agents who had been invited for the personal preview. When they introduced themselves, I greeted them like long lost cousins.

> "It's going to sell and you should be the agent to get that commission."

"Thank you for being here. I was so glad to get your call. Now picture yourself selling this property. It's going to sell and I want you to produce the buyer. Imagine the commission and how your reputation is going to soar, how many more sales will result from being able to say that you sold a property that has been on the market for eight years. Now, I know you've been here many times, but just to refresh your memory, I've arranged for you to go through again quickly. When you're done, don't leave without seeing me. I'll be right here. I value your opinion and I need it. Will you help me to get this sale done?"

One of our open house attendants then whisked them around for a tour. We graciously ignored the fact that, in reality, most had never seen the property; we weren't going there. We just wanted to engage them. Every time any objection was made it was followed by the same empathetic response.

"I know how you feel. I felt the same way when I first saw the property, but it's going to sell and you might as well be the agent to get the commission."

Co-opting feedback

After their tour, I guarded the door like a Buckingham Palace guard. It was most important that they not leave without talking to me. I wanted them to tell me honestly what they thought.

I got what I expected.

THEM: *"It's a lovely property, but they are not serious sellers."*
ME: *"I know how you feel. I felt the same way, but I can assure you they are serious sellers and you should bring an offer so we can demonstrate that seriousness. Do you have someone to whom you can show it?"*

The answer for about ten of the agents was, yes, they did have someone to whom they could show it. Bingo!

Filling the room

The first problem with this property's psychology, the idea that it needed too much work, had been solved. The second problem, that the sellers were not serious, was on its way to being solved. The agents were now at least open to bringing their buyers in to see the property.

We therefore now had traffic and we were filling the room, but this time with buyers.

After the open house, Helen Woodbridge came up to me and announced that she had eleven showings. We suggested she announce this fact triumphantly to her office. Why? Because none of the showings came from her office. Indeed, the gloom and skepticism about the property had been so thick at the firm that few of her agents even came to the open house. Some of this was due to no longer having curiosity about me, having met me at the sales meeting. But largely it was just due to buying into the argument of too much work and the discouragement that comes from believing there is no hope for a sale. I needed her to provide them that hope by telling them of the large number of showings.

By filling the room, I now was able to start controlling the psychology of the sale and it started with the agents in our own affiliate office. Agents, too, need the validation from knowing that others are interested in a property.

Controlling the psychology right at the qualifying

I told Helen that I would personally qualify each buyer and then call her to arrange for the showing. She was delighted that I took this off her plate. In turn, I was happy to talk to each and every agent directly. It allowed me yet another attempt to adjust their attitude and turn them more positive.

The buyers for *Le Domaine Résistance* were like those who come to an auction and find that they are the only ones in the room. The whole listing shouted "sole buyer syndrome." Leery buyers asked, *"Why hasn't it sold in 8 years? What was wrong with it?"* Having overcome the broker skepticism, I now had to work on raising the buyers' comfort level to act and overcome their fear to bid, especially since no one else had bid in eight years.

And how do you get sophisticated buyers to feel more comfortable to bid? You know the answer: other buyers.

Cash offers only, please

Almost every buyer whose agent had requested a showing was qualified and when I spoke with the agent, I was clear what we wanted: cash offers. The property was magnificent and well priced; therefore, I didn't want to bother with time-consuming financing contingencies. I was looking for a cash buyer and a quick closing.

For me, the idea of cash offers and a quick closing was meant to counter two impressions. First, I wanted to tell buyers through the agents that there was no reason for anything but cash offers. Pricing was right, repairs had been quantified, the property was prime and magnificent, and it would sell. It was a good deal.

The second reason for cash offers and a quick closing was due to the suspicion that, if we did not produce a full-price offer with no financing contingency and a thirty to sixty day closing, we might never have a deal. We weren't going to say this publicly but, in our gut, we sensed the possibility of our seller having a change of heart. Because of that we did not want to get the psychology off to a bad start by having agents encourage their buyers to put in offers with contingencies which were not going to create a sale and earn a commission. Anything less than a cash sale with a quick close was just going to waste time.

A little chutzpah can do wonders

Within the brokerage community our chutzpah created a certain shock that was extremely helpful, especially since first impressions are often lasting. The agents soon started buzzing: *"This property has been on for eight years and this guy wants only cash offers with no financing contingency? Boy, he is confident and a little cocky!"* Yes, I wanted to get the property sold, get paid, and get a reputation for being serious. Therefore, why not ask for the order up front? So, I did.

Keeping the audience alert and informed

To control the positive psychology of the brokerage community and overcome their skepticism, we kept the agents constantly informed. The staff used fax machines and snail mail like a blitzkrieg (E-mail blasts did not exist at that time). Initially we sent out a mailing to more than five hundred agents (even to those who didn't attend the open house) just to thank them for their interest. Then we sent another letter telling them that we had eleven showings scheduled for the property and urged them to bring their buyers, too.

What were we doing?

We were continually trying to "fill the room" and ensure that everyone knew it was being filled, especially since unlike in the auction, our room did not allow buyers and agents to see each other. After eight years of unsuccessful marketing, i.e. of the room being empty (which everyone knew), we now wanted everyone to feel the buzz around *Le Domaine Résistance.*

> We new guys were startlingly public in how we sold real estate.

Initially, this constant and continuous communication was a little shocking to the brokerage community. They had never seen anything quite like it. We were trumpeting a stale listing and everyone's involvement in it as if it were the most exciting listing to have ever come to market. Of course, for me (and my team) it was, and we conveyed that enthusiasm daily. Remember, enthusiasm sells real estate.

The agents' initial bewilderment morphed into a kind of weekly fascination with what was going on with the property. Our barrage of letters, postcards, and telephone calls created a transparency that was surprising and then oddly welcome. We new guys were startlingly public in how we sold real estate, which caused everyone to talk about us and, of course, the property.

The orchestration

After every showing I personally called the agent and asked what their buyer thought. Most were positive. Some felt the property was too much for them and the upkeep was more than they anticipated. But, overall, the impressions were positive and led to a conversation I would have over and over:

> **ME:** *"So, will they be making us an offer?"*
> **AGENT:** *"Where do you think this is going to sell?"*

ME: *"It will sell for the asking price which represents clear, defensible value. Do you remember those gorgeous gates? That winding drive? The house, perfectly nestled behind the hill? Do you remember the slight gasp you felt when you entered the courtyard?"*

AGENT: *"But no one is going to bid the asking price! It's been on for eight years."*

ME: Then I asked for the order: *"Give me what your buyer is willing to pay and I will present it and do whatever I can to get a deal done."*

The dialogue always ended with a singular encouragement: *give me an offer*. In the case of this property, an offer was imperative. Why?

Comfort through other bids

Just like the auctioneer needing an opening bid, I needed to establish that after eight years someone wanted this property. The focus had now turned from raising the comfort level and controlling the psychology of the *agents* to doing the same for the *buyers*. I needed an offer within the first four to six weeks of the marketing campaign to raise other buyers' comfort to bid.

Consequently, I was on the phone non-stop soliciting an offer from any agent who had brought a buyer. After all, there had been eleven showings and the brokerage community was now positive about the property. Daily I urged agents to have their buyers throw in a bid.

Given how long this property had been on the market, we had a little more time to get the first offer than the usual two to three weeks. But with this listing, it was even more critical that we produce an offer. Failure to demonstrate that someone wanted the property would confirm all the fears and beliefs of the brokerage community, and showings would trail off. Without an offer, we would be back to the property no one had wanted in eight years.

If, on the other hand, I could get an offer, it would be more than a dose of positive energy. It would be viewed as something close to a miracle, and the audience of weekly viewers would tune in and maybe even cheer on the whole process.

Getting to the first rung of the ladder

The answer was "step ladder marketing." Consider it part of your agent's *power marketing* arsenal. I needed to get to the top of the ladder, the asking price, by starting at the lowest rung, much like the auctioneer starts low to get high.

The starting bid

I got what I needed: a first offer of $550,000, cash, no contingencies, closing in sixty days.

> I first had to establish a base price.

"Well," I thought, *"at least they got the terms right."*

Nonetheless, with this offer, the orchestration commenced. I duly presented the offer to the seller, who duly rejected it. I went back to the buyer, who asked for a counter-offer. The seller countered with the asking price (surprise!) and the buyer balked. I called the agent for the buyer and asked if he would come up in price. He would not. I persisted, but the buyer was done. He would only consider a bargain-basement purchase.

Overcoming sole buyer syndrome

The moment our negotiation ended (it only took a day), we sent out a media blitz. The message was simple: an offer had been made for the property. It was too low to take it, but if you have a buyer interested, please bring them forward now.

My phone rang off the hook as agents called to ask how much the buyer had offered. My response was that since it was still possible that the buyer would come up, I couldn't disclose the price. Then, I turned the focus back to them.

"Do you have someone who wants to make an offer?"

The news of the first offer and undisclosed price spread like wildfire in the brokerage community and helped create dozens more showings. Everyone speculated on how much the offer was for. Helen was asked not to say. I wanted the guessing to continue because it kept the buzz alive and it focused agent attention on the listing.

Calls came from other agents with buyers who wanted to bid. All asked for instruction on where to come in. The response was always the same: only the asking price was sure to take the property.

In about the seventh week a second offer came in. It was for $500,000, $50,000 less than the first offer. Nonetheless, my response was delight. Why?

1) It made the first offer look good and that was hard to do.
2) It was a second bidder, precisely the goal.

Our seller quickly laughed and turned down the offer. I asked,

"What would you like me to tell the buyer?"
"That we already have a higher offer." She said.

That was exactly the response I wanted to deliver and did. I called the initial agent whose buyer had made the $550,000 offer with the news that we had new interest. Did that buyer want to re-enter the bidding?

"They aren't going higher," I was told.
"May I take that to mean our negotiations are over?" I asked.
"Yes," she said.

Climbing to the next step on the ladder

Asking that last question was essential because I would not "shop" any offer, nor did I want to acquire the reputation for ever doing so. As long as the negotiations are still open, I never disclose the price offered. But once negotiations end, I consider it fair to disclose what was turned down. In this case, because I was assured the negotiations were over, I informed the second buyer that we had already turned down $550,000.

> Now I had three offers on the property in two months, and that was three more than anyone had ever known about in eight years.

The agent's response was not surprising. She asked if $600,000 would take it. I told her that to find out, her buyer should make that offer. Her buyer did offer $600,000 and the offer was turned down, as expected. But now I had three offers on the property in two months, and that was three more than anyone had ever known about in eight years. At this point, you can imagine what I did. I called everyone with the news that there had now been three offers on the property. It was this knowledge (widely disseminated by us) that raised buyers' comfort. It is hard to exaggerate how important this is to a buyer. Everyone needs their desire validated and there is no better validation for buyers than knowing other buyers also want what they want.

Speculation continued on the price point and I continued to decline to comment. All I would say to any offer made below the then highest offer was that we already had something better. This process continued for fourteen offers on the property. No need to go through them all, but some increased their increments by fifty thousand dollars and some by

> The psychology of the sale had been successfully controlled and the comfort level of the agents and buyers had been raised by the multiple interest in the property.

twenty-five thousand and some by ten thousand. Throughout the laborious process, I made sure not to violate anyone's confidentiality, but I also made sure that, if the negotiations were ended and the buyer would not go higher, the other offerors knew what had been turned down. *Ad nauseum* I repeated that the only thing that was sure to take the property was full price, all cash, with a thirty to sixty day closing.

In the end, three bidders stayed in the game. Along the way, the number of offers was always disclosed (if not trumpeted). I certainly wanted everyone to know that there was interest, lots of it. A market watching a property that had no offers in eight years needed to see that interest. Surely, I wanted to give every impression of a bidding frenzy.

With each new offer, the comfort level of existing and new buyers was raised by the presence of other bidders. What had been established was not just that someone wanted this property, but four buyers wanted it, then eight, and then twelve, and so forth. The psychology of the sale had been successfully controlled and the comfort level of the agents and buyers had been raised by the multiple interest in the property. Everyone was pulled up the rungs of the ladder with the hope that someone would want to get to the top. The eight-year marketing curse of *Le Domaine Résistance* had been broken.

Hitting goal

In the end, three buyers bid simultaneously and $995,000, all cash, closing in thirty days took the property. We had done what the agents said was impossible. *Le Domaine Résistance* was a marketing triumph with the core lessons of *power marketing* learned. Its sale served to establish our reputation on the North Shore. Within three years, my firm was doing almost half of the top ten sales in that market.

> Everyone was pulled up the rungs of the ladder with the hope that someone would want to get to the top.

The Takeaway

- By quantifying in advance the work to be done, objections were contained and comfort cultivated.

- The "room" for this property had been empty for too many years; the first job was to "fill the room" with interested agents, followed by buyers.

- Interest was revitalized and piqued by inviting, reaching out and cajoling everyone in the brokerage community to participate in the sale, and insisting a sale would occur.

- By encouraging any offer, a low bid was obtained that helped establish that someone wanted this property.

- The initial low bid changed the psychology of the sale. The property was now one that someone wanted, psychologically enabling others to enter the bidding while I kept "filling the room." I then brought buyers and their agents up the rungs of the ladder to generate additional offers.

- The presence of multiple offers was key to raising the comfort level of each additional buyer (and the agents) to bid higher.

- A room now filled with buyers allowed orchestration of bidding to get to one all-important point in time: multiple buyers bidding simultaneously.

- Constant communication with the brokerage community publicly notifying them of additional people in the room at every step kept the momentum and psychology of the sale positive.

- The sale demonstrated that smart buyers indeed pay, but only when their comfort level is raised by knowing others are bidding, too.

Chapter 13:
Sales that explain it all - Clarendon Court

My second *power marketing* story comes from listing Clarendon Court, the magnificent and notorious home on Bellevue Avenue in Newport, Rhode Island that belonged to Martha ("Sunny") and Claus von Bülow. This story perfectly illustrates how having just the *threat* of competition through an orchestrated *power marketing* campaign can be enough to sell a property and even produce a record price. It also demonstrates how smart, sophisticated buyers will gladly pay more, even a record price, when presented with clear, defensible and demonstrable value with a discount attached.

This twenty-room mansion was featured in the opening aerial shots of the 1956 Hollywood movie, *High Society*, starring Bing Crosby, Frank Sinatra and Grace Kelly. The house was built in 1904 by the noted architect Horace Trumbauer who also created the neighboring estate, "Miramar," and the fabled Newport "Elms" mansion. Clarendon Court is an exact copy in design and measurements of

Hedley House, County Durham, England, built by Colin Campbell, the architect of Buckingham Palace.

In December, 1980, this Newport "cottage" was the scene of an alleged murder attempt on Mrs. von Bülow. The two children from her first marriage to Prince Alfie von Auersperg, the Princess Annie-Laurie von Auersperg and Prince Alexander von Auersperg, suspected their stepfather, Claus von Bülow, of trying to kill their mother with an overdose of insulin. An insulin-encrusted hypodermic needle was discovered hidden in a black bag in Mr. von Bulow's bedroom closet.

> Because of so many celebrated aspects, Clarendon Court remains one of the most famous properties in the world.

His 1982 trial, covered daily by the world press, resulted in his conviction and a sentence of thirty years in jail. However, upon appeal in 1985, based upon a search warrant not having been issued when the contents of the black bag were tested by state officials, Mr. von Bülow's legal team, led by Harvard law professor Alan M. Dershowitz, argued that the only possible way for the hypodermic needle to have become encrusted with insulin was if it had been deliberately dipped. This suggested that von Bülow might have been framed. Given the reasonable doubt that had now been inserted into the case, on June 10, 1985, the jury acquitted him of the charges.

Of all the properties that I have handled, Clarendon Court was the highest profile. Because of so many celebrated aspects, it remains one of the most famous properties in the world. Indeed, novelist and *Vanity Fair* reporter Dominick Dunne called Mrs. von Bülow's saga "one of the most sensational stories in the annals of American and international high society."[15] There would later be a movie version of the events, *Reversal of Fortune*, with Jeremy Irons as von Bülow (for which he won an Academy Award) and Glenn Close as his wife, Sunny. Dunne's television episode on the event would replay for years in his TV series "*Power, Privilege and Justice.*"

I listed the property on behalf of the family early in the spring of 1988. Given its fame, Clarendon Court should have had an enormous market of would-be buyers. But the property's upkeep ran almost a million dollars a year. The fact that an attempted murder was alleged to have been committed in the master bedroom created a worrisome psychological impediment. The concern was that the combination could send the property in the way of so many Newport estates: a donation.

Pricing Clarendon Court

To prepare for the listing presentation my LandVest team and I had to figure out what the property might be worth. We followed the exact process described in Chapter 4, reviewing the plot plan, walking the boundaries, and cataloging the rooms and outbuildings as well as the amenities. We began with the underlying land value. To determine a value where there was pre-

> Dominick Dunne called Mrs. von Bülow's saga "one of the most sensational stories in the annals of American and international high society."

cious little if any vacant land, we made a list of sold properties that had been bought and torn down, presuming that the buyers bought them for their land value. We also looked at parcels of land currently available even if they were outside of Newport, but still oceanfront. With all this distilled, we came up with an underlying range of value for the land.

We then calculated the replacement value of the house, the improvements, outbuildings, and amenities. We adjusted for age, use and condition and came up with a Core Value range of values. We then compared this range of value to about five years of property sales in Newport over one million dollars. Not surprisingly, it was not a long list. Research indicated no record of a sale over $1.8 million, and no previous sale was comparable to the magnificence of Clarendon

Court. We then looked at and compared the property to others currently available.

In pricing the property we had many concerns. Was Newport ready for a record price after the stock market crash of 1987? If so, was Clarendon Court the property with which to achieve it? Given the $1 million a year to maintain the estate, would there be any buyers at all? And from a brokerage point of view, would our sellers be willing to accept the market's verdict? Claus von Bülow really did not want the property sold at all. He and Mrs. von Bülow had meticulously furnished it and he preferred that it be retained. Their daughter, Cosima, seemed to feel the same, but was ready to go along with whatever was decided. The two von Auersperg children wanted it sold, not appreciating the continuing glare of the headlines. There was no financial necessity; even the one million a year to maintain the estate was not a problem. Thus, the client, like so many luxury homeowners, had no urgency to sell.

Given the challenges, if any property needed *power marketing*, this was it. The market was tiny and tepid; concerns and doubts were high.

Our considerations

Since this would be one of the most intensely reported and closely watched sales in America, it also ran the risk of being the most widely watched failure in America. We were worried that with the press's spotlight on the property, we, as its agents, might risk highlighting a possible failure. After all, we wanted our name associated only with success.

> Since this would be one of the most intensely reported and closely watched sales in America, it also ran the risk of being the most widely watched failure in America.

In the end, we wagered that given what the family had been through, they would not want the additional stigma of nobody wanting their property. Certainly, a failure would make tabloid headlines of the first order and cause more family drama. We conjectured that the family was committed to getting out of the spotlight and putting it on someone else. In effect, we were wagering that the property's very fame and notoriety would not allow for a public failure, and therefore, a sale at some price would occur. If we could demonstrate a broad-based, all-out, professional effort to find the few buyers out there and get them bidding at the same time, we hoped that all the parties would listen to the market we had created and act accordingly. Such speculation and hope was our team's order of the day.

Determining the core value of Clarendon Court

In evaluating the Core Value, we noted that the land consisted of about seven acres with 680 feet of high stone walls covered in espaliered yew that ensured privacy from Bellevue Avenue. There was also 750 feet of direct water frontage on Narragansett Bay. There was the matter of the tourist walkway "Cliff Walk" between the ocean and the estate's backyard— but fortunately, it had been built below the property to prevent trespassing, preserving the privacy of the owners. That added value.

The von Bülow's also had purchased an adjacent property, "Gull Rock," once a rambling Queen Anne style cottage, which they demolished to provide not only a sweeping vista of the ocean, but a broad golf hole which could double as a croquet course. The Gull Rock parcel was a separate lot that could be sold without interfering with the integrity of the main house, thereby providing additional flexibility and added investment value.

So what was the land worth? There had been some waterfront land sales (without houses) along the coast that had approached $1M. Therefore, we assumed the land was worth a minimum of $1M with a high range of probably 40 to 60 percent more or $1.4M to $1.6M. Given the location and a possible sub-dividable lot, we settled on $1.5M—low by today's standards, but considerable back then.

The house was a three-story English Georgian home in Palladian style built of stone masonry with steel I-beam construction and a copper roof. At the back of the house was a colonnaded open veranda facing a pool and the ocean. The house—almost twelve thousand square feet of living space—had a grand marble stairway with elaborate wrought-iron balusters capped in mahogany. The second floor had two bedrooms in each of two wings, and the third floor had five smaller bedrooms. On the first floor was the famous master bedroom, where the alleged murder attempt occurred. A perfectly proportioned living room extended from the front courtyard of the house to the ocean views at the back. The dining room comfortably sat twenty to forty for dinner. The proportions and scale throughout the house had a twentieth century sensibility that homes like "Marble House" (several doors to the north) and Vanderbilt's nearby "Breakers" did not.

Replicating the house for less than two hundred fifty to three hundred dollars a square foot was unimaginable. Nonetheless, we put a more conservative replacement value of two hundred dollars per square foot or $2.4 million for just the 12,000 square foot house. Still, our valuation of the house without the land was more than had ever been paid for a property in Newport.

Other improvements and amenities included:

- A two-story Queen Anne-styled brick carriage house with steel I-beam construction, a slate roof and garage bays for four to six vehicles.

- A brick-walled cutting garden in eighteenth century English style containing several thousand bulbs of heritage flowers.

- Extensive mature landscaping featuring Japanese black pines, rhododendron, autumn olive, beech trees and numerous other exquisite plantings that were bordered by privet hedges and Rosa Ragusa.

- A 44 x 105 foot heated pool with working fountains that framed the stunning views to the sea.

The yearly rental income from the carriage house apartments was enough at least to defray the $33,000 of taxes on the property. We valued the carriage house and its five apartments at a low of $300,000 to a maximum of $500,000, settling on $400,000 as an average. We valued the perimeter walls, the plantings, the pool and fountains, and the mature landscaping at a conservative $250,000 to $400,000.

In the end, we took all these ranges and arrived (back in 1988) at a total core value of $4,550,000 to replace what was there, not including the "convenience value" —the premium for its being in move-in condition (as discussed earlier, this has a special value in resort markets like Newport). We put a conservative 10 percent premium for its convenience value, believing it would take at least two years to replicate such a house. This added $450,000 a year, $900,000 in total value over two years. It was a stretch, but it was an accurate stretch.

This brought the total Core Value represented by Clarendon Court up to $5,005,000-$5,450,000 before factoring in the celebrity value, which we guestimated at $500,000. When all was calculated, we felt we could articulate and defend a Core Value of $5,500,000 to $6,000,000.

This did not mean we could get that number. In fact, we felt that such a number would scare the brokerage community and likely hurt the possibility of a sale. Rather, we felt we had a defensible value, something that we could argue credibly to sophisticated and informed buyers. But what asking price for such value?

Determining the asking price

Our value analysis then took an unlikely turn. We focused on guessing how much of a *discount* from the defensible Core Value of $5,500,000 to $6,000,000 a smart

> When you take a discussion of how much a buyer is willing to pay and divert it to how large a discount from book value that buyer is willing to bid, you have taken the discussion to a place where sophisticated buyers like to go.

buyer would pay. Discount? Clarendon Court? Linking this property to the idea of a discount was startling and seemed inappropriate.

But we knew what you now know, that nothing raises the comfort level of a wealthy buyer more than a bargain. By looking at Clarendon Court like a balance sheet of a company, weighing its assets and liabilities to get at its Core Value, we were simulating buying a company for a discount from its "book value." When you take a discussion of how much a buyer is willing to pay and divert it to how large a discount from book value that buyer is willing to bid, you have taken the discussion to a place where a sophisticated buyer likes to go.

> By not just looking at the past sales within Newport (what everyone else was doing and thinking), but by calculating the component, convenience and celebrity value, we had come up with the sales rationale we needed for smart buyers. That it was a most unlikely and unexpected one: selling Clarendon Court at a discount to its "book" or Core Value was ironic but completely in line with how wealthy buyers buy. A discount, we reasoned, is how we would create an urgency to act among the few buyers we expected. ***To get a record price we had to talk in terms of a record bargain***. By doing the Core Value calculation we were able to demonstrate a discount to that value and provide the bargain buyers wanted.

To create the discount and finalize an asking price for the property, we slashed a third off our Core Value, believing it might bring us to a tempting price. At a minimum it was a credible and defensible one. This brought us to a range of $3,630,000 to $3,960,000. In the end, we settled on an asking price of $3.95 million and were ready to go to the family and the bank.

Still, our valuation of the house without the land was more than had ever been paid for a property in Newport.

The listing appointment

The listing presentation was held at Chemical bank in a classic mahogany panelled board room. I was attended by my senior partner, Robert R. Borden III, and the following dialogue tries to paraphrase the listing presentation:

"*The price you will get is a function of the marketing you choose today.*" I then paused to let my words sit heavily on the table. The trust officer who invited us in broke the awkward silence, asking what I meant.

"*Clarendon Court is one of America's premier properties. It has all the potential to set a record price for Newport, but only if the marketing that is chosen today is commensurate with the quality of the property. There is no question about the property, its value, or its renown. The only question is whether the marketing can raise the comfort level of the buyers to a point that they will pay up.*"

Someone asked how do we do that?

"*We will market to and include the whole world through a coordinated campaign that involves the media, all other brokers and agents, a targeted advertising and mailing campaign, and orchestrated showings.*

"*Once those buyers are found—and for this property they will be found—everything will turn on whether we, as the marketers, know what to do with those buyers. Our focus will be not on the easy part—the worldwide involvement—but the aspect that requires real expertise: orchestrating the comfort level of multiple buyers to bid all at the same time.*"

I then explained that the market for Clarendon Court was extremely small. That fact would make the buyers nervous about resale someday and about whether, upon a resale, they would be able to recover what they paid. I explained that it was our job to help them overcome their nervousness by presenting a defensible value, and then to create comfort by demonstrating broad interest and competition.

Filling the room with coordinated, sequential showings

I explained our marketing strategy. In order to demonstrate multiple buyer interest, we would arrange showings so that each would have one hour for an initial appointment, and most buyers would see other buyers coming before and after them. For instance, the 11:00 a.m. buyer would see the 10:00 a.m. buyer leave and then see the 12:00 p.m. buyer arrive. In this way every buyer would be aware of the others and recognize that they were not alone. The whole point was to make sure that all buyers knew there was competition and that the room was filling up. More lengthy and intensive second showings would be allowed after the first. We would follow the same strategy on the second showings, if there were any.

I then explained that, in order to get the buyers bidding simultaneously, we would set a date for showings to commence some six to eight weeks after marketing began. This meant that no one could view the property until the showings began, nor could anyone buy the property during the six to eight week marketing period. Borden then explained that we usually dubbed this "Coke Bottle Marketing." In this phase, a day is set for the property to come to market, cooperation and compensation are offered to all agents, and mailings, advertising and public relations commence. All this effort was the equivalent of shaking the Coke bottle to generate a fizz of interest in the property.

We also explained that everyone wants something more when they cannot have it. By indicating that no purchase offer would be entertained until the end of the Coke bottle marketing period, we would pique buyer interest and then set a date for receipt of all written offers. In this way we would funnel interest into a forced narrow decision-making window of time. The showing and decision-making process would, in effect, replicate the room of an auction house where bidders would not be allowed to buy something until they became aware of one another's presence. That instilled the fear of loss. But their awareness of other buyers would provide comfort, too, knowing that others wanted the property. That knowledge combined with a set date for the bids would create the urgency to act that every luxury property needs in order to be sold.

Borden then announced that we had renamed this strategy "Champagne Marketing" in honor of Clarendon Court. There would be the same shaking of the marketing bottle during the initial six to eight week period, but, in this case, it would be a metaphorical Champagne bottle that would pop at the end of the marketing period, hopefully with a flurry of offers and a celebrated sale, complemented by some caviar.

Everyone smiled. We had not planned that phrase; it seemed to come to Borden as we sat at the table. In hindsight, it provided exactly the kind of customization of the marketing process appropriate for such a special property, and its originality pleased everyone, especially me.

Up to this point, we never talked about pricing. Rather, the whole focus of the presentation had been on marketing. Then we were asked to address the pricing issue.

> Our recommended asking price represented a one-third discount from this core value, but nonetheless it was 2 ½ time higher than any prior sale and a new record for Newport.

"We have spent considerable time pricing Clarendon Court, and we recommend an asking price of 3.95 million dollars," I said. *"We think it is a credible and defensible asking price. But remember, the selling price will not be set by us, but by the market. The price you get is a function of how good a market we create."*

I then explained that we had thought through the valuation and wanted to position Clarendon Court with an intrinsic Core Value of almost $6M, pointing out that our recommended asking price was a one-third discount from this Core Value, but nonetheless it was 2 ½ times higher than any prior sale and a new record for Newport.

"We will start to raise the comfort level of the buyers by articulating this demonstrable value and focusing them on the discount. We also

think we can sell this discount to brokers and the press. In this way, we can control opinions on the record pricing in a positive way."

Around the table, heads began to nod. Eyes glanced at other eyes. Some whispers started along the side. Borden was asked whether he concurred in this asking price. He said he did. An attorney stated slightly incredulously that we were talking about getting almost $2M more than what others had said to expect. Reminding him again that price is a function of marketing, I said,

"We think our marketing will get you the highest price. Whether it is 3.95 million dollars or lower or higher will be determined by the market. But we know how to create markets and orchestrate them to get successful results. We strongly feel that 3.95 million dollars is a credible and defensible price and we're ready to go with it."

There was a long pause, followed by some whispered comments around the table while our team sat silently. Then the trust officer who had invited us to present, thanked us for coming. We said goodbye and left the room, not knowing what the verdict would be. The next day I got a call with the news that we would be listing Clarendon Court.

Marketing preparations

To begin the marketing, we spent a day at the house to gather visceral details, such as how the light came through the windows and at precisely which hours. I tried to get the feeling of the house, the emotional senses it gave off so as to better highlight these features when talking with agents and buyers. We also hoped that focusing on such information might deflect questions about the alleged murder attempt.

We framed a dozen potential photographs to feature in the brochure, without invading the privacy of the family or providing anything salacious for the media.

We hired one of our finest photographers, Michael Mathers, known for his *Architectural Digest* shoots. He did exemplary work with lighting which was critical because we were shooting in the low light days of late winter. For a winter brochure, we normally would have looked to dusk or evening shots with light coming out of the windows. Such shots would take the focus away from the extraordinary yet colorless plant life. But Mathers wanted to emphasize the sea, the long stretch of backyard that led to it, and the existing light within the house. Such photography required day shots.

Mathers' solution was to air brush in the missing color, which resulted in a stunning cover featuring the afternoon sun bathing the back of the house, contrasted with the green of the lawn and shrubs and the blue of the pool. One hardly noticed the leafless trees and the empty, dark flowerbeds.

The von Bülow family approved all the photographs and copy describing the property. In the end, we produced a tasteful and non-invasive brochure that captured the emphasis on the details of the property without compromising the privacy of this famous family.

Power marketing begins

In order to shake the Champagne bottle, the brochure was sent to our buyer mailing lists and to thousands of agents around the Northeast and as far away as Palm Beach, Washington, and Beverly Hills. The network evening news carried the story of Clarendon Court and the press covered it worldwide. Helicopters hovered overhead to show the house on the cliffs and the expanse of land. The story of the two trials, however, was recounted in the media *ad nauseum*. Advertising was placed in all the major publications and timed to come out over the course of a month. We solicited the brokerage community so that they would feel part of the sale. We called high profile agents directly; local and regional agents received a personalized letter inviting their

> The rules of the process were made clear to all.

cooperation. Anyone with a bona fide buyer would receive a private preview, and every agent making an inquiry received a detailed articulation of value.

Additionally, the rules of the process were made clear to all: the Champagne Marketing campaign would go on until a specified date — some four weeks out. Then, with the bottle vigorously shaken, the first day of showings would be sequentially scheduled-one hour apart, starting at 10:00 a.m. and ending at 3:00 p.m. All would be clustered into 2-4 days, back to back, with hopes for "accidental" overlap. We would continue until all buyers had their first showing. We would offer interested buyers a more extensive second showing, customized to their needs but within the daily 10:00 a.m. to 3:00 p.m. time frame. We also indicated that second showings might occur with the representatives of other buyers present, such as inspectors, contractors, financial counsellors. We wanted everyone to feel as much competitive "buzz" as possible. Finally, every buyer and agent was told that we would set a time and date for all offers to be submitted in writing and delivered to our offices. All offers would have to make clear the contingencies, if any, and be accompanied by a good faith deposit of 10 percent of the offered price. The family would then decide to whom they wanted to sell, for what price, and on what terms.

> The showings were tightly organized and coordinated as much as possible to make sure everyone knew of everyone else's interest.

Our outreach on all fronts, locally, nationally, and internationally worked. There were some fifteen requested and coordinated showings and every one of the potential buyers had been thoroughly vetted and deemed qualified. Five of the fifteen interested buyers arranged for second showings. Throughout, the showings were tightly organized and sequentially coordinated as much as possible to make sure everyone knew of everyone else's interest. *Power marketing* was off and running as we began to fill the room.

The *power marketing* Last Call

After first and second showings were completed, we called the buyers or their agents to inform them that we had fifteen potential bidders. We then set the date, a Wednesday, for all bids to be in. Setting the date and forcing all interest into a narrow window when that interest hopefully explodes, was the "Champagne Marketing" part of the *power marketing* process. It is only possible with extraordinary properties like this one and was wholly appropriate here.

Then we made the Last Call to every buyer-agent that had expressed any interest or to whom we had shown the property. We asked each to call their client and tell them this was the Last Call. In testimony to its remarkable power, I learned later that, alerted to our Last Call through his buyer agent, one of the bidders increased his offer by $250,000. Is there any doubt that making the Last Call is one of the most important actions an agent can perform to get the highest price?

> Setting the date and forcing all interest into a narrow window when that interest hopefully explodes, was the "Champagne Marketing" part of the power marketing process.

On the Wednesday deadline, I was to come to the bank at 5:00 p.m. and meet with the children, their attorneys and trust officers to present the bids and discuss them. All offers were due by 4:00 p.m. on that day.

Enter disaster

From Saturday to Wednesday, I was alternatively elated at how well everything had gone and anxious about what the buyers would bid. On the appointed day there was an apprehensive quiet around our Park Avenue offices.

Apprehension, however, started to morph into concern, when, by 3:00 p.m. no offers had arrived. At 3:30 p.m. the building's front desk rang my assistant, Sheila Johnson, asking her to come down because there were some people outside with lots of equipment. She came back upstairs to say that there were two television crews waiting on the sidewalk for me to emerge with the bids. Now concern quickly metastasized into panic because with television crews waiting for bids, I was faced with the fact that there were none.

> The most celebrated sale of the decade was now turning into a disaster. And I was orchestrating it.

At 4:01 p.m., with the deadline for offers officially behind us and none in hand, I faced our worst nightmare: the prospect of leading a notorious real estate marketing failure. The panic that settled in brought forth visions of my luxury marketing career going up in smoke and my firm's reputation tarnished—if not incinerated. The most celebrated sale of the decade was now turning into a disaster. And I was orchestrating it.

Feeling ill, I took the men's room key and walked out into the corridor. As I passed the elevators, I saw a messenger with a helmet and cycling gloves waiting.

"Who are you waiting for?" I asked.

"I have a letter package for a David Mi—sha-now- ski or something like that."

"Give it to me," I demanded anxiously.

"My instructions are to wait until 4:10 p.m. to deliver it and it's now only 4:05."

I grabbed the package out of his hand, ripped it open. Out of the envelope I pulled a crisp one-page offer for Clarendon Court, written on fine linen stationery, elegantly signed with a fountain pen. There were no contingencies. The offer was $4.2M cash, closing whenever the family desired. It was from a buyer and an agent that we knew were serious and credible.

"YES!" I screamed. "Four point two. No contingencies. We have our buyer."

Our receptionist burst into tears. Everyone gathered around with a sigh of relief, knowing that they had a job for at least a little while longer.

We called the bank to confirm that I would be there at 5:00 p.m. sharp. The front desk called again to say the reporters were blocking the entrance and we needed to give them what they wanted or ask them to leave.

I put on my coat, tucked the offer into my briefcase, and smiled to everyone with lots of pats on the back. I asked my assistant to call Bob Borden in Boston, *"Tell him the sun is shining in New York and in Newport."*

Outside I stopped for the reporters. With cameras rolling and their microphones in my face, I simply said: *"I have no comment. If the family chooses to make an announcement it will come from them."* I knew they would not likely find them. Safely in a taxi, I sped off to Rockefeller Center to meet with them, their trust officers and attorneys.

Delivering the bid

Apprehensively, everyone gathered at the bank at 5:00 p.m. sharp. I again sat at the head of the long mahogany table.

"I have good and bad news," I began. *"The bad news is that we have only one offer. The good news is that it is for $4.2 cash with no contingencies and from a buyer we have checked out. He is serious."*

Relief swept over the room, followed by smiles and applause.

Clarendon Court closed in August of 1988 to a buyer from Washington, D.C. who came through a referral to a local agent, Robin Corbin of Preferred Properties, from Edward Lee Cave, an esteemed broker in New York with a boutique firm that bore his name. Throwing the net as far and as wide as possible and including everyone in the sale had worked: a New York agent referred a Washington buyer to a Newport agent. You never know from where a buyer will come.

An asking price articulated as a discount to Core Value had appealed to a sophisticated and knowledgeable buyer. Such credible and defensible pricing helped to achieve a record selling price by allowing a very smart buyer to appreciate getting a bargain. Careful orchestration of the sale, especially the Last Call, raised the buyer's comfort to bid $250,000 beyond the asking price.

> We provided the threat of competition so that someone was comfortable (and smart) enough to bid aggressively.

In the end, we had created a market for a property that many believed had none, and out of respect for the intelligence of the would-be buyers, we provided the threat of competition so that someone was comfortable (and smart) enough to bid aggressively.

That December the buyer invited me to an event in New York to give me a gift as a memento of his Clarendon Court purchase. I, in turn, asked him a question that had been bothering me: *"Why did you have the messenger wait until 4:10 to present your offer?"* His response was that he feared that there would be so many offers (read competition) that he did not want his offer shopped to them by arriving too early.

The buyer's fear of potential competition confirmed that, in the absence of multiple buyers, the threat of such competition alone was adequate enough to get a record price. It also raised his comfort level to bid higher than the asking price. It did not hurt that he was also a sophisticated and savvy buyer who was accustomed to paying up for things of quality.

As if this sale needed a postscript, an additional offer came in several days later after the winner's bid had been accepted, offering "10 percent higher than the highest bid." The offer was rejected by the family and their attorneys because it came in late and they felt the offer may have been cleverly intended to dislodge the winning buyer, who had respected the rules. They feared that to consider a second offer after the first had been already accepted might result in so angering the first buyer that he might not sign a contract, leaving the family at the mercy of the second. Having eliminated the competition, the second buyer might then lower the price to be paid. Accordingly, the family went with the first buyer.

But the tardiness of the second offer was revealing. It showed that the second buyer wanted to know if there was competition before he offered an even higher bid. In order to pay an even higher record price, the second buyer needed his desire and judgment validated. In addition, the phrasing of the belated second offer was noteworthy. Clearly, the offer was worded in a way designed to overcome or eliminate the competition. *Power marketing*'s threat of competition had worked and produced the highest price Newport had ever seen (and a second offer that was even higher).

To this day, the buyer is pleased with the record price he paid. More than twenty years later, he still lives in this magnificent property. We spoke with him while writing this book. He confirmed no regrets despite being the person who paid the extra $250,000. The threatened competition had raised not just his comfort level to bid higher, but perhaps more importantly, it resulted in his winning the prize. For such buyers winning is remembered long after paying the highest price is forgotten.

> Power marketing's threat of competition had worked and produced the highest price Newport had ever seen.

The Takeaway

- Value was researched, determined, articulated, and then discounted to generate interest from value-conscious buyers.

- To fill the room the Champagne bottle was shaken vigorously through blanket offers of cooperation and compensation to agents everywhere and complemented by direct mail, advertising and public relations marketing.

- Buyer demand was demonstrated through the staggered and tightly orchestrated showings, creating both fear of loss and raising the comfort of buyers by validating the wisdom of their interest.

- Urgency to act was created by funnelling interest into one moment in time when buyers would have to submit their bids.

- The Last Call provided a smart and highly sophisticated buyer the rationale needed to pay more than the asking price (with delight) and to win the property.

- Only after interest and desire had been validated by the winning offer, did a second even higher offer materialize. The second offeror required competition in order to act, and then craftily worded his offer to try to eliminate it.

- By instructing the messenger to wait until 4:10 p.m., the winner, too, attempted to diminish the competition expected from the carefully orchestrated threat. But competition or the threat thereof got the highest price.

Comments? Contact us.

Linda@PowerMarketing.pro

David@PowerMarketing.pro

Appendix 1: About our "2-3 times" definition and why we use "Average" vs. "Median" price to define luxury real estate

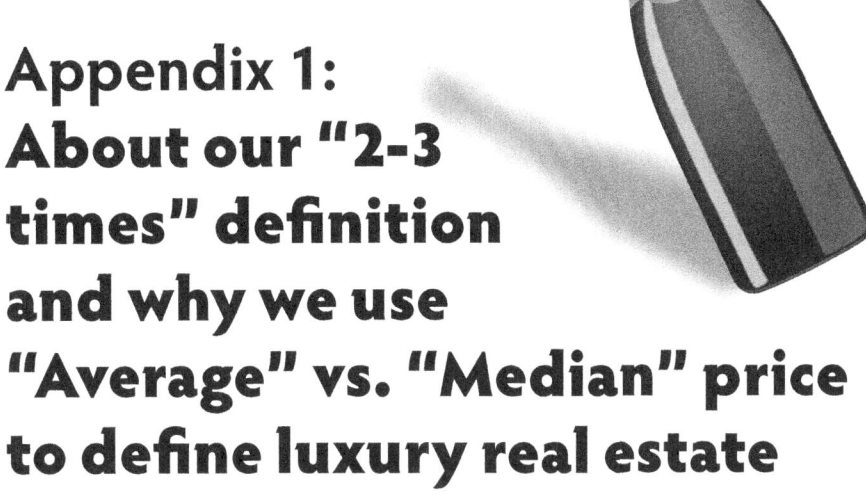

Our definition for luxury real estate is both objective and subjective. The objectivity is provided by the mathematical part of the definition, "2-3 x the average price." The subjectivity comes from the qualifier, having the "requisite qualities" of a luxury property.

Subjective requisite qualities could include: originality, rarity, celebrity value or history. They could consist of spacious bathrooms

Luxury real estate = 2 – 3 x the average price in a market + requisite qualities.

or designer kitchens. Or, the property may have a truly outstanding address, tremendous land for the area, or breathtaking views. Perhaps, too, it has architectural details or exquisite decorating that may be beyond what is considered normal in its market. In general, requisite qualities are attributes that set the property apart from others.

Developing a sense for the requisite qualities

To develop a sense for "requisite qualities," we suggest looking to publications such as *Unique Homes, The Dupont Registry* and *Architectural Digest.* In addition, many local markets have their own home and lifestyle magazine to showcase the best of local good taste. These magazines (and websites dealing with luxury real estate) can help to develop a sense of the "requisite qualities" pertinent to your specific local market.

While this book is about the core *power marketing* skills to sell a property for the highest price, to understand and define luxury real estate the local market's "requisite qualities" must be known. We leave it to you and your agent to learn them.

Why we prefer "average" vs. "median"

We prefer to use a definition for luxury real estate of "2-3 x the average price" instead of the median price.

The "median" is the price point where 50 percent of the properties trade above and 50 percent below that number. "Average price" is calculated by taking all the sales in a market, totaling their value, and then dividing that summary value by the number of sales to arrive at an average. Both are reported by the National Association of Realtors® and most local Multiple Listing Services.

If we were to use 2-3 times median price as our base criteria, several things happen. First, we end up statistically not very far from the same place as the "*top 10 percent definition.*" That gets us right back to having millions of homes counted as "luxury" that are not, the total of which far exceeds even the most generous calculation by the Federal Reserve and the Census. It thus drops our price point and trivializes the exclusive nature of luxury real estate.

Some agents like to use median rather than average price because it is not affected much, if at all, by the occasional periods when a few sales at the extreme end of the market allegedly "skewer" the average price. As this argument goes, the average price can be too affected by such sales; therefore, it does not give an accurate reading on the market. The median price, however, gives little consequence to and is only minimally affected by such extreme sales.

The fact that average price is affected by such occasional large sales (and median is not) is the very reason that we *prefer* to use it.

True, if we have a $40M sale in Greenwich, it absolutely skewers the average price by pushing it up. We would argue, however, that by skewering the average price upward, such sales raise the bar—thereby making it more challenging for properties to fall into the "luxury" category under our "2-3 times average price" definition. We want those big sales factored into our definition because they often set a new standard for a market, reflecting new plateaus that buyers are willing to pay. We want our definition to be sensitive to such raised bars and new plateaus and only the average price accommodates that. We would argue even further that such sales also raise the expectation of what a luxury property is in any market.

Thus, we feel luxury is best reflected in average price and marginalized by median price. By using average price, we keep the definition of what constitutes luxury luxurious.

If we are confronted with those circumstances where such a skewering by one or two sales of the average price truly distorts the representation of even the high end of the market, possibly because there might be so few luxury sales at one time in one market area, this significant discrepancy usually lasts only for one or two quarters–or at most four. An agent should be able to adjust a presentation when this occurs and explain what the skewed data represents, e.g., a once in a lifetime $40M sale in a market where the average might be only, say, $1.3M. In addition, an agent can always smooth out such averages and look at them in the longer term context of six months or one year.

Our definition

We have found that the "2 x average price + requisite qualities" definition best applies to the most luxurious and liquid markets (Beverly Hills, Manhattan, Greenwich, the Hamptons, and Palm Beach) and we prefer a definition of "3 x average" for lower priced and less liquid markets.

A study of those most liquid markets above shows about 12 percent to 15 percent of the buyers annually seek out a "2 x average price" home or higher. This amounts to one in every 6-8 buyers. If we use "3 x average price", it would be around 9 percent or one in every eleven buyers. Remember, this is true only in a handful of towns that represent the largest, most liquid markets. That's as big as the luxury market gets.

Let's assume that we create an index for a market that utilizes a multiple of 2.5 x average price and apply it to some different markets.[16]

Manhattan, New York: In 2008 the average price was $1,590,000; therefore, any property over $4,000,000 would initially qualify. By 2010 it had dropped to $1,350,000; therefore any property over $3,300,000 would qualify. In 2012, it came in at $1,450,000, making $3,750,000 and above a luxury apartment.

Greenwich, Connecticut: In 2012 the average home price was $2.3M; as a result, the luxury end is over $5,000,000.

Beverly Hills, California: In 2010 the average price was $3,066,734, making luxury real estate initially defined as over $7,500,000.

Hollywood, California: In 2010 Hollywood enjoyed an average price of $1,030,000, making luxury real estate anything over $2,500,000.

Palm Beach, Florida: In 2009 the average single family home sold for $3,400,000; as a result the luxury market would be made up of sales over $8,500,000.

Dallas, Texas: In 2010 the average sales price was about $420,000; therefore at 2.5 x average price the luxury market would be those homes over $1,000,000.

Lancaster, Pennsylvania: With an average price of $270,000, a property would qualify for being in the luxury real estate market if it were likely to sell for $675,000 or more. If there are none, so be it.

Endnotes & Citations

1 Thomas Hobbes, *Leviathan parts I and II* (New York: Bobbs-Merrill, 1958), p. 68.
2 U.S. Bureau of the Census, U.S. Census of Population and Housing 2000 (Washington, D C: Government Printing Office, 2000). We are still trying to get updated information from the 2010 Census.
3 Brian K Bucks, Arthur B. Kennickell, Traci L. Mach and Kevin B. Moore, "Changes in U.S. Family Finances from 2004 to 20087: Evidence from the Survey of Consumer Finances," Federal Reserve Bulletin, 95 (February 2009), A-1-A-55.
4 In 2004 Zhu Xiao Di, a Harvard researcher issued a study titled "Million Dollar Homes and Wealth in the United States." Using the million-dollar benchmark as a dividing line, he tried to calculate how many luxury homes existed in America. See his excellent report Zhu Xiao Di, "Million Dollar Homes and Wealth in the United States," Harvard University's Joint Center on Housing Studies, January 2004, page 2.

5 This figure includes condominiums and multifamily, whereas the U.S. Census data only uses "single family owner-occupied" to define the overall market.
6 We are compiling evidence from the field and we will update our website with the new findings at *http://www.PowerMarketing.pro.*
7 Kirk Henckels, "Luxury Residential Report, Overview of the 2008 Luxury Market," Stribling & Associates, January 1, 2009, p1. Accessed August 13, 2009 at *www.stribling.com.*
8 Josh Barbanel, "At Long Last, a Leveling Out?" *New York Times*, September 27, 2009.
9 For a discussion of rapport building and the oblique way to speak to foreign buyers, see David Michonski and Carol Weinrich, *Global Connections: Marketing Homes Internationally*, at *http://PowerMarketing.pro*, due fall 2014.
10 "Profile of Home Buyers and Sellers, 2000," National Association of Realtors, October 2008.
11 Indeed, on this score your chances have improved to 1 in 25 because of the 11% of the sellers who sell their homes without using a real estate agent, about 37% of those (4% of the whole) sold it to someone they knew. See "Economist's Commentary," March 12, 2008, "FSBO Sellers Decreasing" by Jessica Lautz, National Association of Realtors, Chicago. See also, "Field guide to working with FSBO's: Most Important Reasons for Selling Homes as FSBO," where 27% of FSBOs sold to a relative or friend and 14% had the buyers directly contact them as noted at *http://www.realtor.org/library/library/fg2109* (accessed on October 9, 2009). The percentage dropped slightly to 37% where 26% sold to a relative/friend/neighbor and 11% had the buyer contact them directly. See *http:///www.realtor.org/library_secured/library/fg2010* as accessed August 12, 2010.
12 According to NAR "The median selling price of an open-market FSBO home was $185,000, while the median price for all agent-assisted sales was $215,000." This is better than 15% more for the agent-assisted sale. Date is updated as of March 12, 2010. See *http://www.realtor.org/press_room_secured/public_affairs/tpfsbo.* Accessed August 11, 2010.

13 Obviously, we are not recommending what percentage commission should be charged, rather we are saying that premium service and expertise are worthy of a premium commission.
14 Throughout the dialogue in these last two chapters, we have utilized the technique of writer's license to reconstruct dialogue as faithfully as memory serves.
15 Dominick Dunne, "Sunny Memories," *Vanity Fair* online, January 30, 2009.
16 We are in the process of creating a luxury marketing index. It will be released on our website, *http://PowerMarketing.pro* and *http://GetYourHighestPrice.com*.

Other products that might interest you

- For a Free **Directory of Market Experts**
  Go to *http://GetYourHighestPrice.com/Directory*

- For a Free **Quarterly Market Report on the US market**
  Email us at: *Report@PowerMarketing.pro*

- To purchase a subscription to the **Core Value Pricing Calculator**
  Go to: *http://GetYourHighestPrice.com/CoreValue*

- To purchase a subscription to the **Home Value Appreciator**
  Go to *http://GetYourHighestPrice.com/HomeApp*

Made in United States
North Haven, CT
28 February 2025